THE BIBLE AND AMERICA

THE BIBLE AND AMERICA

Larry Braidfoot

BROADMAN PRESS
Nashville, Tennessee

Dewey Decimal Classification: 261.9
Subject Heading: CHURCH—GOVERNMENT POLICY—
                              UNITED STATES
Library of Congress Catalog Number: 82-073371
Printed in the United States of America

To my parents,
Amie Lee Braidfoot
and
Leonard Dow Braidfoot,
Who taught me about honesty and compassion
Without which goodness in life and government
will not long endure.

Introduction

If you have been asleep for ten or fifteen years, like Rip Van Winkle, you will find things have changed greatly when you wake up. This is especially true in the area of American politics.

The Vietnam War finally ended. Both a president and a vice president have resigned under clouds of suspicion. Gerald Ford succeeded to the presidency and was recognized for his contribution to the restoration of confidence in the integrity of the office. Yet he was defeated by a relatively unknown Georgian who did about as much as Billy Graham to make the phrase "born again" familiar throughout American Society. Jimmy Carter, whose religious faith was such an integral part of his public image, was in turn defeated by Ronald Reagan, at least partly because many Christians who had voted for Carter in 1976 turned to Reagan in 1980.

Now if you were not asleep during all of this, and were following the political events of the last decade, you are aware that one topic of considerable conversation is the involvement of Christians in politics. There has been a strong resurgence of interest in politics among Christians of America, especially in some of the conservative circles where involvement had been quite low. This resurgence has been greeted with mixed reactions. Some voices of praise have been raised, others of criticism.

Americans are, by and large, a religious people. Many of our founding fathers were religious people, primarily Christian.

Evidence of religious belief adorns our nation's history and its institutions.

Christians have been involved in politics throughout our nation's history. But at times this involvement has been almost nonexistent, especially in terms of group involvement. A study of American history reflects periods of intense interest in political and social issues on the part of Christians; at other times apathy seems to have been the general attitude. High levels of involvement were seen in the abolitionist movement, the prohibition movement, and the civil rights movement.

Christians who are involved in politics seek to shape American society based upon their understanding of biblical values and principles. Christians are convinced that the Bible, although written centuries ago and in lands vastly different from ours, sets forth some insights which can be valuable to the Christian who seeks to apply his or her Christian beliefs to the world of government.

Christian involvement in politics is not an easy matter; it involves many challenges. It requires the same courage that Christian living demands in every area of life. Two particular challenges seem especially important. First, since our nation is so different from the nations of the Bible, it is difficult to discover the similarity which we would like between that time and ours. As we look for insights in the Bible, we find that we must interpret for ourselves what the Bible is saying about politics and life in community. A second challenge grows out of this process of interpretation. Christians often differ in what they believe the Bible teaches about politics, life in community, morality, and responsibility. Christians are involved in different political parties and frequently assume different positions on the same issues.

One way of avoiding differences of opinion among Christians is for Christians to withdraw from the political process. I don't think that is the avenue to be chosen. Unfortunately, I feel many

Christians have chosen this approach. Instead, I am convinced we must become better students, both of the Bible and of politics. As we understand better what the Bible teaches about God, how he works in nations, and what he expects of those nations, we will then grasp better what we are to be doing. As we learn more about our nation, how it works, and what its problems are, we will be more sensitized to the areas where Christian values can and need to be applied.

This book is written as an attempt to provide some insight into the Bible's teachings and how they have been applied by Christians in American politics. Admittedly, this is not an exhaustive treatment. Several chapters briefly treat subjects which deserve much fuller treatment. It is my hope you will read this book as an introduction to a number of areas deserving far more detailed study.

Chapters 1 and 2 examine the teachings of the Bible regarding government. Chapter 1, which deals with the Old Testament, explores the origin of government, the form of government present in the Old Testament, and the functions of government. Chapter 2 discusses the major teachings of Jesus, Paul, and John regarding government. Some elements of continuity will be noted and specific insights developed, growing out of the Roman setting for those writings.

Chapter 3 analyzes different positions Christians have taken on political involvement. I have found it helpful to group these into four categories, ranging from asceticism and withdrawal to the desire for a theocracy. I believe it is extremely important to see clearly the implications of these different models. As Christians, we have a responsibility for the world, so we need to understand how responsible we are being.

Chapter 4 introduces you to some of the groups which have been established to work in the field of Christian citizenship. These groups provide a variety of opportunities for information and leadership which can assist Christians in their political involvement.

Chapters 5 and 6 relate to the separation of church and state and the danger of civil religion. Perhaps the most significant contribution of America to man's religious life is the concept of separation of church and state. Chapter 5 is a brief treatment of a subject which is far more complex than this short chapter could possibly reflect. Throughout much of human history, such freedom has not been practiced. Christianity, dating back to the Emperor Constantine in the fourth century, has frequently been established in some special relationship with the state. Americans long ago decided that this would not be so in this nation. This is not an easy position to maintain, especially for a religious people. One of the worst dangers is the temptation to engage in civil religion, the subordination of religious interests to the interests of politicians and the state. We will see that even in the Bible, there were constant manipulations of the people's religious life to achieve some political goal. Independence in matters of faith allows the individual to be free of state domination and state manipulation. This freedom must be maintained and practiced.

The last chapter will briefly examine how some Christian values are vital to the shaping of public policy. An entire book could be given to this subject alone. Because my intentions are to develop the teachings of the Bible, I have not given as much attention to historical matters and to present and future issues as some would desire. This is the result of a conscious choice, for I feel that the purpose of this book is to describe a foundation upon which present and future involvement can proceed.

There are many uncertainties about involvement in politics. For the Christian this requires careful thinking and planning. Formulation of strategies may be difficult.

The one fact not open to discussion is whether Christians have some responsibility for the government under which they live. I think God has given us an imperative. The only question is whether we will be loyal to that imperative. If we are, we will discover that God is at work in the political process and simply beckons us to join him. As free creatures, the choice is ours!

LARRY BRAIDFOOT

Contents

1.
Government in the Old Testament

The religion of the Old Testament was often so intertwined with the prevailing political structures that the two seem indistinguishable. To the casual reader, this often leads to the conclusion that the political structures of government are either unimportant or missing. This is especially true to those reared in the United States with its democratic form of government and its elections. But the Old Testament provides a most important foundation with which the Christian can determine how to be involved in political life.

The Old Testament reflects a culture and a setting which are strange to us. The leaders were patriarchal figures, kings, priests, and prophets. Slavery was accepted. Women occupied a position of secondary importance. Life was less complex and so was government.

The teachings of the Old Testament regarding government can be appropriated best by describing the origin and nature of government, the form of government, and some teachings about how government functions.

THE ORIGIN OF GOVERNMENT

Although no single passage gives a systematic description, statements are found in the Old Testament which enable us to speak of the origin of government. From these passages, two broad theories are usually formulated.[1] One theory asserts that government originated in the nature of man. The other theory asserts that government is an institution which was made necessary by evil and sinfulness.

First, the theory that government originated in the social nature of man will be examined. This theory originates in part from general observation and common sense. Human beings like to be around each other. Some individuals prefer to live in seclusion; some are hard to live with. Yet the majority of individuals want to associate with others. The fellowship which we experience provides intense joy, stimulation, and meaning to life.

More than just wanting to live around other human beings, we need other persons. We see this most easily by thinking of the birth process. The infant needs the mother. The mother needs medical care to avoid disease and premature death. The person living in the city needs the farmer who grows the food which is transported by the trucker to the market.

The Old Testament abounds in passages which reflect this social nature of human beings. The very image of God (Gen. 1:27) involves the power and capacity that persons have to communicate, to fellowship, and to interact with other persons. The purpose for which God created man is social, requiring mutual effort at multiplying, populating the earth, and exercising dominion (Gen. 1:28). Man was not intended to do this alone (Gen. 2:18). Both Old Testament and the New Testament view persons only as they are in community with one another. In the Old Testament, man is understood in his relationship to Israel, the people of God. In the New Testament, man's full destiny is seen as a part of the body of Christ, the church. To talk of mankind is to talk of the community to which we are a part.

Community life involves organization. Even before the selection of a king, governmental authority was present. It was the authority of the leader of the clan, the father of the household, or the mighty warrior. The very authority with which God invested man involves the authority to govern the community to which he belongs.

The second theory of the origin of the state regards the state as being a necessity because of the evil and sinfulness of mankind. This is often described as a result of the fall of man. The fear of Cain represents a fear of death from the hands of unrestrained force (Gen. 4:14). Certainly Cain's fear reflects a life alienated from God, but he expressed a fear that other human beings would take his life. He was aware that the community of mankind was broken in fellowship and feared that other persons might kill him unless some authority intervened. Sinfulness did create a new awareness of the need for protection, a protection which is a function of government.

This need for protection easily can be seen in other passages which are more specifically related to government. Judges 21:25 is such a passage. The passage describes a time before the selection of a king and reveals a longing for a king who would establish Israel as the nation which it was intended to be. This longing for a king is understandable if we examine the cycle which recurred throughout the period of the judges. When no judge ruled over the people, the people sinned and only punishment from God moved the people to repent. Lack of leadership—religious and political—presented an opportunity for sinfulness. The remedy seemed obvious—have a king like other nations.

The sons of Samuel were considered unsatisfactory by the Israelites. They did not walk in the ways of their father (1 Sam. 8:4-5). The Bible does not make clear why the Israelites thought that a king would be more faithful to God than would the sons of Samuel. In spite of warnings by Samuel, they sought a new kind of leader.

In this longing for a king, we see not only a rejection of God's sovereign rule over the nation (1 Sam. 8:7), but also a human wish for stability. The desire for a king was a rejection of the type of government God wanted for them. It indicated an expectation on the part of the Israelites that some form of government was the proper way to restrain evil and to deal with external enemies of the nation.

"Man's capacity for justice makes democracy possible; but man's inclination to injustice makes democracy necessary."[2] I would conclude with a similar statement about the origins of government: Man's social nature makes *possible* life in community, which is organized to confer authority upon some individual or group of individuals. Also, the fears and evidences of social evil make *necessary* the organization of government as the only means of preventing social chaos, anarchy, and injustice. Government is a response to the highest aspirations of man and also to his deepest fears.

THE FORM OF GOVERNMENT

The form of government found throughout the Old Testament is the theocracy.[3] This is a government in which God is recognized as the sovereign. The Old Testament unfolds the story of God's choice of Israel as his chosen people. God selected Abraham as the individual through whom he would build a nation to bless the nations of the world. For such a divine purpose, a divine form of government was needed. Only a government in which God was sovereign was sufficient.

God chose to exercise his sovereignty through human servants. At times the ruler was simply the head of a family or clan. In the period of the judges, God used individuals selected at a time of need. Later God allowed the Israelites to have kings, even though this was not his desire. The role of leader was not without risks. Both Eli and Samuel as judges proved unable to control and guide their own sons. Even David, the ideal king, "the man after God's own heart," proved unable to resist the pride and lust which on occasions brought tragedy to the nation.

The first form which God's rule took in the Old Testament is the leadership of the *clan* or *family*. This leadership is found throughout Genesis. It stands out most clearly in the stories of the patriarchs: Abraham, Isaac, Jacob, and Joseph. Each man was responsible to God for leading the covenant family. Abraham exercised necessary force in securing the safe release of Lot and his family (Gen. 14:13-16). He settled an economic dispute between his herdsmen and Lot's herdsmen before bloodshed occurred (Gen. 13:1-13). He set the religious example by his sacrifice to Melchizedek (Gen. 14:17-24) and faithfulness to the covenant. In this manner, Abraham served as a faithful servant of God in establishing the covenant people.

Perhaps Joseph's role as a government figure is even more descriptive of the manner in which God used human servants. Joseph rose to prominence in Pharaoh's court as God exercised control over events in Egypt. He served as an officer second only to Pharaoh in a government which historically engaged in worship of the sun and other nature deities. Yet the power of God enabled Joseph to be a servant of deliverance not only for the covenant people, but also for the Egyptians from famine and starvation. Joseph functioned in a role which delivered not only his family but also a nation which by the time of Moses had returned to worshiping nature deities. Joseph served in a political office which might be compared to the prime minister of England, who exercises most of the governmental authority in behalf of the king or queen. Joseph was clearly God's servant.

The next stage in the development of theocratic government is the stage of the *charismatic leader*. The word *charismatic* is variously used in contemporary Christianity. The word is employed here to describe an individual whom God selects at a point in time for a special role. Neither Moses nor the judges were individuals who by birth or tradition were expected to provide leadership. Moses did not want to serve even when selected by God (Ex. 3—4). But through a method by which only God can ascertain the proper man and persuade him to serve, God brought Moses into a position of monumental importance. In less dramatic fashion, God also selected the judges for periods of crises which threatened Israel.

Moses exercised total authority over the people of Israel. He was the military leader, the religious spokesman, the one to whom God revealed his plans for the people, the one through whom God revealed the many moral, civil, and criminal laws by which the people were to be governed. The Covenant Code (Ex. 20—23) and the Holiness Code (Lev. 17—26) are two important passages which gave guidance to Israel about the total life of the community.

The broad scope of the law which God gave through Moses can be demonstrated by looking at Exodus 21—23. The heart of these chapters is the Decalogue or Ten Commandments (Ex. 20:1-17). These verses lay down in broad form the moral values and guidelines which God sought to establish among his people. These moral values do not set forth specific laws about what is permissible and what is not allowed. They seek to establish basic principles which God expects his chosen people to follow.

Basic principles are often subject to different interpretations. God gave through Moses a more detailed group of laws which applied these bedrock principles to situations with which the people of Israel might be confronted. God did not want ignorance of what he expected to allow for moral license. Exodus 22:1 sets the penalty for theft of livestock. This is an illustration of a criminal law. Exodus 21:33 is a civil statute which prescribes the penalty for the economic harm done to the other man's livestock. Moses did not distinguish between moral, civil, and criminal statutes. But the reader familiar with these different kinds of laws can find many illustrations of all three types throughout the material God gave through Moses.

Moses was an astute military leader. The Exodus is the single most important event in the Old Testament. It symbolizes the power of God to deliver his chosen people and to establish them in their own land. The period of wandering in the wilderness exalted Moses to a position of even greater importance as he was charged with the care, the leadership, and the training of the people for the eventual entry into the land of Canaan. His remarkable leadership was only slightly diminished by his own act of disobedience which prevented him from leading the Israelites into the land.

Moses appointed lesser officials known as judges to assist him. Jethro, his father-in-law, pointed out that Moses was too besieged with duties to be able to handle all of the disputes between the people. Jethro told Moses that the task would wear him out and that it was not good for the people either. So Moses appointed judges who ruled in his place over smaller groups (Gen. 18:13-27). Even though Moses was God's chosen leader, he had to have help.

This diversification of leadership is important. The judges fulfilled not only a religious function but also civil and criminal adjudication functions. Thus early in the Old Testament, the theocratic government began to experience change and growth in administrative structure. Government changed as the needs of the people demanded. The changes were necessary, enabling Moses to serve more adequately in his role as the leader whom God had raised up to deliver the people. The changes did not represent a rejection of God, however. Jethro counseled Moses to act only at God's command (Ex. 18:23). Since Moses did it immediately without the Bible recording any dissent, we must conclude that this modification of the administrative structure of the government had God's blessing.

The role of the charismatic leader as God's representative and servant was continued in the period of the judges. This period of several hundred years was one of alternating faithfulness and faithlessness, of peace and turmoil, of hope and despair. During this period, thirteen different judges exercised leadership. The judges served primarily as military leaders whom God used to deliver the people from bondage to their enemies. These individuals were selected by God without reference to their status in life. God chose the individual whom he regarded as being appropriate to lead the people. The period of military leadership was sometimes followed by a period of service as a judge settled disputes and served as God's spokesman to the people. But upon the death of the judge, no replacement was selected. The people lived without a special leader appointed by God. The Israelites during the period of the judges were an *amphictyony,* a confederation of people united mainly by a common religious belief in and devotion to God, but not by any unifying form of government.

The history of Israel during this period can be summarized as a cycle which was repeated over and over. The children of Israel practiced evil and idolatry, forsaking the worship of God for the worship of pagan deities. God became angry with the people and delivered them into the hands of their enemies. The experience of bondage caused the people of Israel to repent and cry out to God for deliverance. Then God heard their prayers and would raise up a judge who delivered them. The people remained more faithful to God during the leadership and rule of the judges than after their death (Judg. 2:11-23). The absence of a judge became an occasion for license and idolatry.

The feeling began to grow that the precipitating problem was the lack of a leader who would rule over the people continually. Hence at the close of the Book of Judges, we hear the writer say, "In those days there was no king in Israel; every man did that which was right in his own eyes" (Judg. 21:25, RSV).

The next stage of development in the theocratic form of government is that of *kingship.* The office of king brought permanent leadership to the nation and enlarged the responsibility which was to be vested in one individual. For good or for evil, it satisfied the desire of the people for one individual to whom they could look for leadership at all times. The origin of the office of king was discussed in the previous section. Frequent references will be made in the following section to the manner in which the office of king functioned.

Several facts should be noted at this point, however. The method of selection was not clearly established until Solomon succeeded David. It was the desire of Saul that Jonathan succeed him. But because of Saul's sin, his son was not allowed to be his successor. God sought out a man after his own heart, David, who later established his son as his successor. From that time, the normal channel of succession was for the eldest son to become king upon the death of the father. This proved to be more true in the Southern Kingdom (Judah) than in the Northern Kingdom (Israel, which split off at the death of Solomon). In the Northern Kingdom, violence and rebellion frequently led to the seizure of the throne by a new family or dynasty. Succession was quite sporadic and varied.

Although the king had wide authority, we should note that God established a system of checks and balances in his rule over the people of Israel. We must remember that the government of Israel was a theocracy, one in which God is the king who rules through human agents. It is true that the king was one of those agents, but he was not the only agent. Although the king had responsibilities in leading the spiritual life of the nation, he shared those with other individuals.

The priests had increasing responsibilities in directing the worship of the people and providing instruction. At times, the priests became so enmeshed in the affairs of state that they forfeited their independent role. This was true of Amaziah, the high priest of Bethel, who rebuked Amos for proclaiming the word of God in judgment (Amos 7:10-17). The existence of the priesthood and its special responsibilities were to serve as reminders to the king that his authority was limited. The priests performed rituals of worship and sacrifice for which only they were authorized and prepared. The king was not to usurp those functions.

The greatest check upon the power of the king, however, was the prophet. God ruled his people through kings who proved to be all too human in their sinfulness. The king, the one who was supposed to lead, needed frequent correction. God raised up prophets as needed. They were as different as Isaiah and Amos. Some labored as prophets for years, others for months. They shared in common the responsibility before God to speak his word to the nation. The prophetic message usually included a word for the government and the social institutions of Israel. When the religious sins of the people were enumerated, the sins included those committed by the kings and the leading citizens. Sins against other Israelites were always identified. The concerns of the prophets were profoundly social. They wanted the people of Israel to repent and alter their behavior, not merely their acts of worship.

The American system of government is also based on a system of checks and balances. To a certain extent this is true of the government of the Old Testament. The king was the primary authority among the rulers. The priests served the people in worship and sacrifice. The elders provided wisdom for judgment and resolution of disputes. The prophets were God's occasional agents to speak a word of rebuke, correction, or encouragement to the entire nation. God did not entrust his entire purpose for the nation of Israel to one human authority or one institution. He sought to utilize all of the institutions of Israel and special messengers to achieve his goal of peace and justice for the nation.

In looking at the theocratic form of government represented by the kingship, we see how difficult it is to achieve.

The last stage of development in the theocratic form of government is the *priestly* stage. This stage begins to unfold at the end of the Old Testament and grows throughout the intertestamental period.

The Babylonian Captivity caused a reexamination of Israel's faith and of its social institutions. The leaders of Israel during the Exile and on the return to Jerusalem were predominantly priests.

The absence of a monarch during the Babylonian and Persian periods had left a gap in the leadership position. The priesthood grew in strength to provide leadership. One of the last efforts at Jewish independence, the Maccabean Revolution, resulted from the military leadership of a priestly family.

Increasingly the concept of kingship became enmeshed in thought of God's ultimate kingdom. The Messiah as an eschatological figure would establish a new kind of kingdom. He was to be a special kind of king, of the lineage of David but superior to any previous king of that lineage. The eschatological longings of the people were quite strong. As they longed for the era of the Messiah, the authority within Israel came increasingly to rest with the priests. The kings, if they could indeed be called such, were weak. The voice of the prophets ceased. The priests responded to the void by increasing their power. By the time of the New Testament, the priests would represent almost unchecked authority in Judaism.

THE FUNCTIONS OF GOVERNMENT

The next step in examining the role of government in the Old Testament is a look at the functions of government. What does government do? What does it seek to achieve?

The first function of government was to *protect the people of Israel from their enemies.* The leader, usually the king, was judged by his ability to protect Israel. The desire of Israel for a king rested in part with a wish for a leader who would lead them in standing firm against their enemies. Several illustrations highlight this function.

Saul, the first king of Israel, was considered a promising leader. He was endowed with outstanding physical attributes, but his family did not become established because of Saul's sin and eventual cowardice. He cowered before Goliath and endured the taunts of the Philistines. The people of Israel were delivered by the hand of the Lord as David responded to the challenge. From that time forth, David was the foremost warrior. Upon him was the responsibility of protecting Israel. The adoration of the people was given to David because it was he, not Saul, who secured their lands, fought their enemies, and made their homes safe (2 Sam. 5:1-2). Saul's jealousy can be explained in part as a result of David's successfully doing what Saul should have done.

David extended the power and grandeur of Israel to a new high, conquering Jerusalem, extending the boundaries of the land, and subduing the enemies of Israel. He was known as a man of war. In the eyes of the people, he was perhaps the ideal king. Even in his sin, he had a commitment to God which restored him.

We can also see the protective function of government when it was absent. When no leader was able to protect the people from their enemies, their lament was clear. Often the voice of the prophet pointed out the corruption and decay which rendered a particular leader unable to give the people protection. The prophet Isaiah served God at a time when the kings were weak. In chapters 7 and 36—37 he spoke God's word to the leaders, challenging them to pursue policies which would preserve the nation from their enemies. Both in the political crises of 735 BC and 701 BC, Isaiah insisted that the leaders resist turning to foreign powers for assistance, especially Egypt. Turning to other nations instead of to God would lead to destruction.

The Old Testament is clear that deliverance comes from God.

Kings who gloried too much in their success were humbled, not being able to complete their dreams. David wanted to build a Temple to God, but he was not allowed to do so because he was a man of war. A Temple which he built would have inevitably been a monument to himself (1 Chron. 28—29).

Solomon was allowed to build the Temple, but his toleration of and practice of idolatrous worship prevented him from establishing a kingdom of peace and righteousness. He neglected and forgot the ways of God. He also forgot that the king was to be a blessing to the people, not a burden. Although he was successful in keeping the people free from external enemies, his rule as king achieved only that one function. He was not able to achieve other goals which God intended the king to fulfill (1 Kings 11).

The second function was for the government to be responsible for *promoting justice and fairness in the nation*. The king in Israel always held his position by the grace of God. He was not divinely given the nation of Israel to rule over as he pleased. The king was responsible to God for the manner in which he governed the nation.

The requirement of justice can easily be seen in the last public address of David. As he spoke to the people, he began: "When one rules justly over men, ruling in the fear of God,/he dawns on them like the morning light,/like the sun shining forth upon a cloudless morning,/like rain that makes grass to sprout from the earth" (2 Sam. 23:3b-4, RSV). The ruler held office as a representative of God and was bound by God's requirements. He was to make the nation of Israel one of priests, a holy nation.

David was not a perfect man. As he spoke his last words to the people, no doubt he recalled a number of sins: his adultery with Bathsheba and the eventual death of her husband Uriah, the pride of numbering his armies, and the turmoil within his own family which resulted from laxity and inconsistency. David was painfully aware of the costs which had been exacted for his sin. Future

leaders should do better. They should live in fear (awe or
reverence) of God. This awareness of God's expectations required
the king to rule by standards. God had given the law to establish
clearly the responsibilities of the people of Israel. The law gave
clear guidance for religious, civil, criminal, and economic
behavior. The king had the responsibility of leading by example
and of using his authority to assure that the nation followed the
laws God gave. To fail as an example or to fail to require justice in
following God's laws was to fail as a king.

Again the failure of the kings to fulfill this function of
government can be seen in the prophets. Amos cried out for the
establishment of justice and righteousness (Amos 5:24). Micah
reminded the people that God had shown them what he required:
justice, mercy, and loyalty (6:8). God would not protect and
establish the kingship of a ruler who ignored him and his
expectations.

A third function which government existed to serve was the
resolution of conflict among citizens. This arose in the time of Moses
and required the appointment of judges who would serve the
people and relieve Moses for other responsibilities. This need was
too heavy for any one man to perform. This function was
continued in the period of the judges. It was seen in the
background of the Book of Ruth (4:1-12). It explains the function
of the elders meeting in the city gate to hear testimony regarding
disputes. The need for truthfulness on the parts of witnesses was
tied to the importance of the rulers being able to resolve conflicts.

A fourth function of government in Israel was the *promotion of
the worship and service of God.* Throughout the Old Testament the
leaders of families had religious responsibilities for the belief and
behavior of their families. The rulers had even greater responsibilities—whether they were judges, kings, or priests—of leading
the people to worship and to serve God. No leader could be an
adequate ruler if he only protected Israel from her enemies. The

political peace which might result could only be sustained if the people as a whole were loyal.

David again emerges as the model. Although his personal sins had an enormous impact upon the nation, he is remembered as the man and king who was "after [God's] own heart" (Acts 13:22). I like to think that David's life was characterized by a repentance which served as a model for all of Israel. Having sinned, he repented and sought again to be loyal to God. The Old Testament does not portray David as going after foreign gods. He did not, as Solomon did, build shrines for other gods.

Other kings are not portrayed as being as loyal to God. Saul, in a time of severe need, sought a word for his future from a medium (1 Sam. 28). Solomon allowed his many wives to entice him into tolerating and perhaps worshiping foreign gods (1 Kings 11:1-11). Manasseh is described simply as having done that which was evil (2 Kings 21:2).

The kings of Isaiah's time sought to establish peace through treaties with foreign powers. Since such treaties involved a recognition of the power of those nations' gods, those alliances amounted to a denial of God's sufficiency for Israel. The kings during the time of Amos and Hosea engaged in formal ritual and ceremony which was empty and did not change the character of the people. Lives were not transformed, evil was tolerated, and indifference was rampant.

The worship of God cannot be separated from the service of God. Acts of worship must issue in acts of service and moral behavior. Amos found unacceptable the worship which allowed an individual to oppress the poor and deal deceitfully in economic matters (Amos 5:10-15). God has given ethical standards. He expects his people to abide by them.

A fifth function of government was to *use the authority of government to protect the poor and the oppressed.* Perhaps nothing was more foundational for the government of Israel than this. Before giving the Ten Commandments to Israel, God reminded them, "I am the Lord your God, who brought you out of the land of Egypt, out of the house of bondage" (Ex. 20:2, RSV). God premised his Commandments on his prior act of deliverance and Israel's awareness that they were former slaves who had been delivered. As former slaves, they should know what oppression was like. As former slaves, they should be grateful for their deliverance. This deliverance from bondage was to be the motive and basis for their service of God and their fellow man.

The Old Testament recognized the institution of slavery. But God was teaching his people as rapidly as possible that it was wrong. He did this by teaching them that slaves were to be treated humanely. They were to be liberated after a period of years. They could not be abused and mistreated as in other nations (Ex 21:1-11).

The year of jubilee was designed as a time for economic recovery and restoration. In an agricultural land, those who did not possess land were subjected to poverty and deprivation. Every fifty years, the land was to revert back to the original family. Failure to observe the year of jubilee resulted from acceptance of economic practices of Canaan and other lands which regarded the land as a private possession, to be used at the sole discretion of the owner. This was in direct conflict with the understanding that the land was a gift of God to the people of Israel.

Leviticus 25 and 26 describe in powerful fashion God's expectations of the people. In these chapters his expectations of care for the poor and the oppressed are spelled out vividly, as well as the punishment which is to follow from failure to obey. The description of the year of jubilee and its liberation of slaves and those suffering from economic want vividly portray God's expectation that the authority of government support these practices. If the Commandments of God are not followed, if the people of Israel do not serve him, the leaders have failed. If the judges, kings, prophets, priests, and elders are loyal to God, the entire nation will follow this leadership.

The government which neglects the widows, the orphans, the weak, the helpless, the oppressed, and those who have no advocate to defend them cannot be considered a government which follows the model of the Old Testament.

2.
Government in the New Testament

While government and religion in the Old Testament are heavily intertwined, government in the New Testament remains in the shadows. The primary focus of the New Testament is on the life and ministry of one central figure, Jesus of Nazareth, and his followers.

Jesus and his followers had frequent contact with affairs of state. Jesus was born while Mary and Joseph were traveling to fulfill the requirement of the Roman government that an enrollment for taxation be conducted. Jesus was crucified at the order of a Roman governor. Paul was imprisoned in a Roman prison and exercised his rights as a Roman citizen, appealing to Rome for a legal decision. John, the author of Revelation, was in exile at a time when persecution by Rome had begun.

But the New Testament does not have many direct teachings about government, its nature, and its duties. It is possible to extend the teachings of the Old Testament by examining the passages and by looking at other passages which indirectly reflect an understanding of government and its role. In this chapter, the different forms of government reflected in the New Testament will be described. Against this background, the direct teachings of the New Testament will be examined.

FORMS OF GOVERNMENT

The Jewish people were controlled by several different systems of government at the time of Jesus. The dominant political authority was not Jewish but Roman. The fact that the highest authority and greatest power was foreign was not unique in Israel. This had been true since the time of the Babylonian Captivity. The Jewish people had been dominated by the Babylonians, the Persians, the Greeks, and eventually the Romans. Only a short period of independence under the leadership of the Maccabees offered the possibility of Jewish control of their own political and social institutions. This independence was broken finally when the Romans asserted their superiority about 63 BC.

The *Roman* government exerted a broad, yet relaxed, influence over the Jewish people. Rome did not seek to control every area of the life of the conquered people. The religion of the Jewish people was recognized as legitimate, and the people were allowed to continue their forms of worship without Roman interference. The Romans required the payment of taxes and obedience to the laws and rulers of the Roman empire. But this domination allowed a place for the Jewish people to maintain their uniqueness as a people of faith.

The Jews of the time of Jesus bitterly resented the presence of Roman influence. Jewish theology emphasized the uniqueness of Israel and their possession of the land of Palestine as their special inheritance, "their Holy Land." The presence of a domineering group of people conflicted severely with the Jewish expectation of what life should be. Thus the Romans were generally hated. Strife and enmity existed, although usually in latent forms. Eventually this enmity would flare in rebellion, so that Jerusalem was ravaged and laid waste by Roman soldiers in AD 70.

The *Sanhedrin* was the court which exerted the highest authority allowed to the Jewish people. It exercised authority in various matters at the discretion of Rome. It functioned primarily as a religious council, making decisions related to religious matters among the Jews. Since considerable freedom of religion was allowed, the Sanhedrin's influence was significant.

Among the Jews, four different religious groups, which held widely different views, may be identified. Each of these groups espoused views which expressed specific thoughts about the role of government. The groups were the Sadducees, the Pharisees, the Essenes, and the Zealots.

The *Sadducees* were a group of aristocrats, small in number but powerful in influence. They influenced through position and wealth. They were not as closely associated with the commoners as were the Pharisees. But their wealth and position allowed them to have a strong voice in shaping Jewish policies. They were well represented in the Sanhedrin. The Sadducees tended to be sympathizers with the Romans. They generally advocated a position which would maintain the status quo and would accept the domination of the Romans. We can easily see how their friendly posture toward Roman domination was a result of their economic status. The Roman government had established and maintained peace throughout the Mediterranean. In this atmosphere of restraint, commerce and trade could be conducted with relative safety. Revolution was not likely; social upheaval was resisted. So the Sadducees could enjoy their privileged status and maintain their economic affluence without serious threat. The key to their continued influence was their success in persuading the Jews to remain passive in their acceptance of Roman domination.

The second group of Jews was the *Pharisees*. The Pharisees were more legalistic, more nationalistic, and more closely associated with the common Jew. The Pharisees were not as aligned with economic interests as were the Sadducees. Rather than possessing the wealth of commerce, they busied themselves with affairs of worship at the Temple and with teaching the Jews to observe and follow the law of Moses. The Pharisees looked fervently toward the coming of the Messiah. They thought that God would send the Messiah as a national leader who would vanquish the Romans and reestablish the kingdom of David. The Pharisees were quite nationalistic in their expectations. The resentment of the Romans which was seen in many Jews was present in their attitudes. They simply controlled it in the service of the law. Revenge would come in due time as God would send his Messiah as a powerful soldier-king who would vindicate the Jews and give them the political freedom for which they longed.

The third group of Jews was the *Essenes*. They represented a dramatic withdrawal from the world. They lived in communities withdrawn from the normal occurrences of life. Their emphases tended to be nonpolitical and to focus on personal righteousness. Rather than pinning their hopes on a Messiah who would be a soldier-king, they expected the coming of a teacher of righteousness who would lead them in the purity which God desired. The ascetic tendency represented by the Essenes would eventually lead to the establishment of Christian orders of hermits and monasteries. In those Christian institutions which would develop several centuries later, the spirit of withdrawal would become complete. The affairs of the world, including its government, would be abandoned to those who had chosen to live amid worldly concerns. Government to the Essenes with their ascetic tendency was unimportant.

The fourth group was the *Zealots*. This group perhaps took government more seriously than any of the other groups. They were so zealous that they wanted to throw the Romans out of their land by force. The Zealots were militant nationalists who were seriously offended at the presence of the Romans and at the humiliation of the Jewish people. They abhorred the sympathizing tendencies of the Sadducees, they discounted the patience of the Pharisees in waiting for the Messiah. They sought answers other than the withdrawal chosen by the Essenes. They wanted to find deliverance in their own time by the use of force, if necessary. The Romans could not be tolerated any longer.

The appearance of any popular figure who might be a leader

sparked the concern and curiosity of the Jews. Perhaps a person appearing from nowhere and announcing himself as a servant of God might be the Messiah who would restore the nation. Maybe he would be the dynamic leader who could spark a rebellion of force. Even the Sadducees, who did not long for such a leader, had to regard a new figure with interest because of his possible threat to the status quo which they sought to maintain.

Jews of New Testament times carried over the general teachings of the Old Testament regarding government and its relationship to their faith. They were vitally interested in their own form of government, and in order to attain that government, they had to achieve independence.

It was into this kind of environment that Jesus of Nazareth was born and in the midst of which he came as an adult in his public ministry.

JESUS: RENDER UNTO CAESAR
WHAT IS CAESAR'S

Jesus lived a public life in full view of the political and governmental leaders of Palestine. He appeared before the Sanhedrin, before Herod, and before Pilate. None found actual fault with him; he was convicted of no real crime. Yet he suffered a cruel, political death which could be ordered only by a Roman official.

Jesus had frequent contact with Gentiles and unimportant Jews. He was willing to associate with and to minister to individuals who were looked down upon by orthodox Jews who had close association with the Roman government. The gospel was good news to these rejected individuals. Their acceptance by Jesus was preshadowed in the preaching of John the Baptist. In the beginning of John's ministry, at the very time John encountered resistance and opposition from many Jews, soldiers asked him what they could do in response to his preaching. These were the Romans, hated and despised by most Jews. John simply told them to avoid violence and wrongdoing (Luke 3:14).

Early in his ministry, Jesus encountered a Roman centurion and healed his servant. The faith of the centurion was commended as superior to the faith that Jesus had found among the Jews (Matt. 8:5-13). In neither case was condemnation offered for being a soldier in service of the Roman government. The only concern was with the personal morality and faith of the individual and with the manner in which the individual acted as a soldier. Faith in God and repentance were compatible with one's involvement in the Roman army.

In addition to Roman soldiers, Jesus associated with publicans or tax collectors. The story of Zacchaeus is a model of how Jesus related to them (Luke 19:1-10). He did not demand that they renounce their relationship with the Roman government. By the response of Zacchaeus and the words of Jesus, we can see that the quality of life and personal faith was Jesus' interest. Jesus thought it possible for an individual to be loyal to God and loyal to the Roman government. Not only did Jesus associate with these tax collectors; he called one to be a disciple (Matt. 10:3). Jesus, in his acceptance of them, attracted enough tax collectors for the Jewish religious leaders to accuse him of associating with them as well as other sinners (Matt. 9:10-11).

This same Jesus who associated with Roman soldiers and tax collectors, who moved freely about the land without opposition from Roman officials, attracted opposition from the Jewish leaders early in his ministry. The Sadducees and Pharisees were disturbed by his ministry and by his acceptance of Romans on an equal level with Jews. The Gospels clearly show that for most of his public ministry Jesus was followed closely by representatives of the Sadducees and Pharisees who sought some offense with which to accuse him. They yearned to levy an accusation against him which would justify having him executed (Mark 3:6).

One effort to trap Jesus provided the context for his most direct statement about government. We cannot fully appreciate his statement without seeing the motives behind the question Jesus was asked. The Master was near the end of his public ministry, and the Pharisees still had not been able to find anything with which they could charge him. So they set what they thought was a trap. They sent representatives to Jesus, but those representatives went to Jesus in conjunction with the Herodians, a group of Roman sympathizers. They were Jews but held positions of influence because the Roman government had given the Herodian family delegated political authority to rule over Palestine.

The Pharisees would be incensed if Jesus expressed ideas too sympathetic to the Romans. The Herodians would be irked if Jesus did not appear to be loyal to the Roman government. Regardless of his answer, the Pharisees felt he would be trapped. The question: Is it lawful to pay a tax?

The answer Jesus gave provides a simple yet profound perspective with which the Christian can examine his or her responsibility to government: "Render therefore to Caesar the things that are Caesar's, and to God the things that are God's" (Matt. 22:21, RSV).

Jesus asked for a coin to be used in paying the tax. The coin in question was a special one used to pay a poll tax. It was payable by an individual and differed from property taxes on commercial transactions. On the coin was a picture of Caesar. The coin was one of the symbols of Roman power, and possession of the coin by the Jews was an indication that they had accepted in fact the rule of the Romans.

Jesus in his response surpassed the question. He went beyond the legality of paying the tax to the morality which required that it be done. The word *render* means "to give back." Payment of the tax was simply a giving to Caesar something to which he was entitled. The payment of taxes by a Jew would be his contribution to the maintenance of the Roman empire, its army, and the peace it preserved. The Jewish people benefited from this peace. They might not like the Roman rule, but it had some benefits for them.

As long as the demands of Caesar did not conflict with one's duty to God, obedience was morally required. Jesus indicated by his simple statement that it was indeed possible for conflict to exist. It was possible to render unto Caesar that which he was due as long as it was also possible to render to God that which he expected. We know from the teaching of Jesus that total loyalty can be expected only by God (Matt. 22:36-40). As long as Caesar did not infringe upon the opportunity of the individual to serve God, Caesar was due obedience.

In this manner, Jesus affirmed both the legitimacy of the Roman government and its limitations. To the Pharisees, Jesus affirmed the moral duty of obeying this foreign government. Government was not limited in its legitimacy to government which was Jewish. To the Herodians, Jesus indicated the limitations which all governments have. They are not to exalt themselves to the position of expecting unqualified loyalty. God is the only one who can expect total, undivided, unqualified allegiance. Any government which demands for itself this loyalty is elevating itself to the position reserved for God. This is civil religion in its basest form.

In this simple teaching, Jesus suggested the manner in which the citizen lives with a dual citizenship. The citizen has a double loyalty. The greatest loyalty is due God, but loyalty and obedience to the government under which one lives is a moral responsibility. Having received the benefits of that government, the citizen is to perform the duties which are expected by that government.

Jesus had the opportunity of being king. During a popular stage of his public ministry, the crowds sought to seize him by force and make him king (John 6:15). He was constantly suspected of seeking to become king of the Jews. If the concept of theocratic government could ever have worked, it would have been with Jesus as the king. But Jesus had already rejected the possibility of being a king of the sort recognized by the Jews. The temptations in the wilderness (Luke 4:1-13) all involved temptations to be a ruler or king by the standards of the Jews and of the world. Jesus was tempted to use his power for his own gratification and to set his goal on attaining control of the world's kingdoms. He was also tempted to display his power before the leaders of the Jewish people so they would recognize him as their king. All of these he refused. Jesus would not let himself be made king because he had already rejected that role for himself.

Jesus not only rejected the possibility of becoming king himself; he did not reinforce the Old Testament concept of a Jewish theocracy. According to that concept, God was recognized as king and the human king was simply his representative. Jesus did not affirm that concept in his teachings. If silence is taken as disagreement, then Jesus by his silence disagreed with the concept which the Jews accepted. Certainly the silence of Jesus concerning that form of government stands out in contrast with his acceptance of the system of Roman government under which he lived.

Those who would seek to establish a theocratic form of government in our world cannot claim a teaching of Jesus to support that goal.

PAUL: BE SUBJECT TO A GOVERNMENT OF TOLERATION

If Jesus affirmed in general the authority of the Roman government, Paul demonstrated how to live with the benefits of Roman citizenship. Paul, a Roman citizen, lived with a dual citizenship—the citizenship of Rome and a spiritual citizenship based on Judaism. He utilized his Roman citizenship to the fullest, enabling him to promote the spiritual vision with which he was blessed.

Paul functioned fully within the culture of his times. He accepted a number of practices which have subsequently been questioned. He accepted the institution of slavery and advised a slave (Onesimus) to return to his master (Philemon). He ministered in a world dominated by males, and he advised women to remain silent in church gatherings to avoid offending unbelievers who might be present (1 Cor. 12). In these and other ways, Paul sought to be "all things to all men, that I might by all means save some" (1 Cor. 9:22b, RSV).

Paul the evangelist traveled extensively throughout the Mediterranean region. His trail left evidence of his ministry, as individuals and churches sprang up from Jerusalem to Rome. Perhaps no man traveled more extensively than Paul, enjoying the fruits of the peace secured by the Roman legions. Paul appears to have traveled in relative safety, attesting to the effectiveness of Roman rule in maintaining law and order.

Paul did not experience the same intensity of persecution which would develop within a matter of decades. Jesus implied that Caesar might make demands that conflicted with loyalty to God. The Book of Revelation describes the persecution which resulted from the demands of emperor worship. But that idolatry had not yet occurred in the time of Paul.

Paul was persecuted, of course. But the persecution was from the Jews. Paul (then Saul) was a catalyst in the early persecution of Christians, but later, after his conversion, that persecution was turned on him. The Roman Empire recognized as legitimate the national religions of the conquered nations, the adherents of those religions were not persecuted. During most of Paul's life, Christians were considered a sect within Judaism, and as such they were protected. Only when persecution by the Jews thrust with finality the followers of Jesus outside of Judaism did

Christianity become recognized as a separate religion and lose its legal status.

Paul's clearest teaching about government is found in Romans 13:1-7. This passage is set in a broad context in which Paul is giving advice about living in social relationships. He warns the readers against doing evil to others, urging them instead to overcome evil with good and to live at peace with all people (Rom. 12:17-21). He follows with an emphasis on loving one another; love does no wrong to the neighbor and fulfills the law (Rom. 13:8-10). His teachings about government are offered as a rationale for how one should do good in relationship to civil authority.

Paul did not tolerate lawlessness. He cautioned against lack of respect for and obedience to civil authority. He urged his readers to recognize that civil authority is of God. All authority is given by God. This is implicit in the doctrines of creation and providence. God even uses rulers of pagan beliefs for his purpose (Isa. 36—37).

God established the authority of government to serve his purposes. Our examination of government in the Old Testament disclosed several purposes which were to be served, including the restraint of evil and the establishment of peace. Those who would resist authority oppose one of the means which God ordained to establish peace among men. The principle of authority requires subjection. Without authority to which all are subject, the result is the same as in the latter days of the judges—"every man did what was right in his own eyes" (Judg. 21:25, RSV).

Paul clearly would not require subjection which violated one's duty to God. Although he did not repeat the words of Jesus about rendering unto God that which he was due, their meaning was clearly present. He described the type of ruler to whom subjection was owed. The ruler to whom subjection was due simply required the citizen to do that which was good. Those who engaged in good behavior had no need of fear from the rulers. Only those who engaged in evil had cause for fear. Indeed, those who did good would be praised by the rulers whom Paul described.

Rulers should be a cause of fear and terror only to those who did evil. To them, the ruler should be a source of fear because of the sword of authority. They wield the sword of authority to restrain those who do evil. The ruler is a "minister of God" (Rom. 13:4,6) both to those who do good and to those who do evil.

Why were (and are) rulers to be obeyed? Two reasons were given. They were to be obeyed both for the sake of conscience and for the fear of wrath. To those who acted out of conscience, good behavior was clearly a recognition of the ruler as a "minister of God" to preserve order and harmony in society. To those who were tempted to do evil, the ruler was a "minister of God" who caused them to restrain their evil tendencies through fear of the punishment.

How were rulers to be obeyed? Each person was to be subject to the governing authorities. The same word was used as in describing the manner in which the church is subject to Christ (Eph. 5:24). The church is subject to Christ because he is the Lord who has redeemed the church and has proven himself trustworthy and loving. Failing to be subject to this kind of love would be denying one's relationship with Christ which is the essence of faith. Only two reasons could explain failing to live in subjection to the ruling authorities. Either the individual must be intent on doing evil or the ruling authorities must be contradicting the purposes God intended.

Subjection to the ruling authorities required several things. The most specific form of obedience was the payment of taxes. Paul was most specific with the question of taxation because it was of special importance. Payment of taxes not only involved a transfer of money. It also became a means of support of and participation in the tasks which the government performed. It was an act which symbolized acceptance of the ruler's authority. In this passage, the words of Jesus echo.

Paul talked about custom, fear, and honor. He gave specific instructions to render or to give these things to those to whom they are due. Give them to no one to whom they are not due, but to everyone to whom they are due. Obviously some interpretation was called for, but it clearly indicated a sense of limits. Render only what was due to Caesar (government). The teaching had a double meaning. To those who would be free of government, whether Roman or otherwise, Paul communicated a duty to be subject. To those rulers who might be tempted to expect more or to those subjects who would give more to ruling authorities than they were due, Paul's words were commands not to give that which was not due. Only God is worthy of total loyalty. Any person or institution—church, state, or family—which expects more is to be resisted.

Paul's words have been interpreted as requiring obedience to any and all governments. This is seen in the Lutheran tradition by the manner in which German churches in the 1930s supported, or at least did not openly oppose, Adolph Hitler.

The theology reflected in that passive acceptance was a theology which was deterministic. Since Hitler was in power, God must have willed that he be there. Since God apparently willed that Hitler be in power, only God could remove him from power. Until God did, the church was bound to obey him. This type of interpretation of Romans 13 seems to go beyond the intent of Paul. He did not address the question of how the Christian responds to an authority who, by his acts of hatred and genocide, violates God's purpose for government. Paul had yet to begin experiencing the persecution that the church later went through. For insight into that problem, the Christian must look elsewhere.

Several passing observations are called for. First, Paul did not concern himself about the form of government. He made no efforts to shape his words so as to express a preference for one form of government over another. In Paul's teachings, some of the seeds of individualism and equality are found. For example, he asserted that in Christ there is no distinction—sexual, national, or racial (Gal. 3:28). But he did not develop this into a preference for a form of government which was democratic. Although he expressed thoughts about equality, he did not develop a theory of individual political rights. He accepted at face value the legitimacy of the government with which he was familiar, a monarchy headed by an emperor. Second, Paul did not qualify his teaching in any manner for the religious belief of the ruling authorities. He was neutral on the religious belief of the rulers. He focused on how they ruled, rather than why they ruled in that manner. Apparently a non-Christian ruler could act in a manner that satisfied Paul's expectations. His concern was for the result of the ruler's exercise of authority.

Paul made it plain that the rulers of the world will pass away also. Paul noted the role of the rulers in crucifying Jesus. Both Jewish and Roman rulers were involved in the crucifixion. They did not have the mature wisdom which Paul desired for the believers (1 Cor. 2:6-8). For this reason, Paul advised the Christians to refrain from lawsuits, but to settle their disputes among themselves (1 Cor. 6:6-8). Christians were to pray for rulers so that the believers would be able to live quietly and with godliness and dignity (1 Tim. 2:1-3).

The state to which Paul counseled subjection was a state which practiced religious toleration. Rome did not confer, at this point in time, full freedom of religion. But in practice, Paul had all of the religious freedom which he desired. He felt no restraints upon his service of God as he traveled not only through Palestine, but also throughout the area of the Mediterranean. The mystery religions, the Roman popular religions, and the state national religion were widely practiced. In this period prior to the advent of persecution, religions such as Judaism were tolerated. To Paul, the state was a secular institution. It was ordained of God, but it did not have a specifically religious function. Embodied in his attitude toward the state was the expectation that there were some standards of morality and behavior. Some things were good behavior. Other behavior was evil. These were to be praised or punished by the state. In so acting, the state acted as God's minister, even if it did so unknowingly. The state did not have the function of promoting religion. Paul accepted the reality of his day, without any nostalgic longing for a Jewish theocracy. If Jesus simply ignored the Jewish theocracy as an option for government, Paul moved a step farther away from it.

Paul probably did not concern himself more specifically with some of the questions of vital interest today because of his eschatological beliefs. Paul seems to have expected Christ to return in his lifetime. In 1 Thessalonians 4 and 5 and in 2 Thessalonians 2, Paul gives indication that he expects an imminent return. In 1 Corinthians 15:51, Paul stated that not all would see death. Since he expected Christ to return very soon, he busied himself with the task of proclaiming the gospel. He sought to evangelize the whole world in a flame of energy that seemed unquenchable. He simply did not take time to speak of some things which are important to those alive nineteen centuries later. He gave himself to that which he regarded as most important. For other things such as his attitude toward government, he gave us sufficient clues to have some insight into the will of the Father.

JOHN: PASSIVE RESISTANCE TO A GOVERNMENT THAT PERSECUTES

In the latter part of the New Testament era, the state became a persecutor. For several reasons Roman policies toward Christianity changed. First, Christianity became recognized as a separate religion, distinct from Judaism. As such it lost its protected status as a national religion. Second, Roman emperors began to require that they be worshiped as divine. The earlier practice of recognizing emperors as divine after their death was changed to accord that status to them while alive. Worship of God as revealed in Jesus Christ could not be tolerated.

The shift which occurred in Roman policies was a shift from toleration to persecution. The response of the New Testament shifted from one of subjection to passive disobedience. It was no longer possible for the Christian to render to Caesar those things due Caesar, because Caesar now left no room for the Christian to render to God that which God was due. The Roman Empire sought to command total, undivided loyalty, which presented a direct conflict with the teaching that the believer was to have no one, or no cause or no institution, before God.

The church lived with a growing tension. The believers were to recognize that political authority was ordained of God and to pray for the rulers (1 Pet. 2:13-17 and 2 Tim. 2:1-3). But as persecution began to grow, they were ever mindful that their ultimate citizenship was not in this world (Heb. 11:10; 13:14). Faced with the choice of worshiping the emperor and thereby disobeying God, the early Christians anchored themselves more fully to the promise of a destiny in a city whose maker and founder was God. This they would not compromise. They would endure persecution passively. They would be martyred. But they sought to remain firm.

The most important passage which delineates the Christian response to persecution is found in Revelation 13. John was in exile. With all of the power of his imagery, he warned against giving in to the demands of the beast. The beast which troubled John was the Roman Empire, but the power of his image offers words to those persecuted by both past and future nations which seek to exalt themselves above the God of history, who gives them their existence and their authority.

The clearest part of John's message was his advice to the saints: persevere. Endure persecution and go to captivity if you must. Faith in God was demonstrated by perseverance in time of crisis and persecution. Those who had heard the word spoken by God would hear the warning and stand fast (Rev. 13:9-10). The imagery was broken with the simplicity of John's call to obedience. Those who have chosen to obey God will understand.

John's imagery has evoked extensive analysis and discussion. Extensive analysis of the entire chapter is not required. It is possible to extract certain basic insights to demonstrate John's position about the persecution of the Christians.

Within the chapter, two beasts and a dragon appeared. The dragon was Satan, who gave authority to the sea beast, the Roman Empire. The government of the Roman Empire sought to conquer the whole world and to subject it to obedience. The government of the Roman Empire sought to establish itself as a totalitarian regime which could command undivided loyalty of all its subjects. It sought to have the total obedience of all its citizens/captives and to supply any needs which it regarded as necessary. It sought to be regarded as wonderful and without equal.

One tangible way to assure the allegiance of those ruled was to require their worship. Those who worshiped the emperor indicated their loyalty and acceptance of the totalitarian regime. Those who refused to worship the emperor indicated that they could not be trusted to be loyal and subservient. They were to be persecuted. Here government, ordained of God, had been given a new direction and goal by the authority of Satan. The result was a distortion, so that those who sought to do good by God's standards were to receive evil.

The Roman Empire created a religious establishment to further these goals. Worship of the emperor required priests and magicians. Magic and signs were used to convince those who might need convincing.

Totalitarian governments exist only to serve the needs of those who rule. They misuse the power of those governments to further their own ambitions and objectives. They crush those whom they should serve as God's ministers.

Any union of government and religion is subject to distortion. Where religion serves government, civil religion is dominant. The goals are the goals of the state. The voice of prophetic dissent is absent. The norms are the norms of the elite. The enemies of the ruling elite are the enemies of the state and its gods. A religious motive for disapproval and persecution exists. This was true in ancient Israel, as in the days of Amos. It was true in the first century, as in the Roman Empire. It is still true today.

The government, ordained of God, which practiced a degree of toleration, had now become a government of persecution. For the Christian, the only path was that of disobedience.

3.
The Christian
Hope for Society

The apostle Paul identifies hope as being one of the major qualities of the Christian life. In describing the supremacy of love, he nonetheless mentions that hope along with faith is an abiding quality (1 Cor. 13:13). The Christian hopes for many things related to the world in which he or she lives. He or she hopes for the advance of the gospel, for growth in personal holiness and righteousness, and for ministry to those in need. The Christian also has hopes and aspirations for the society in which he lives because God is the creator of all persons and the one who ordains all government.

The Christian not only has goals and aspirations for society, but also has hope for it. Hope is born of previous actions. The Bible gives testimony of God's involvement in societies of old and his activity for the redemption of the individuals and the society of which they are a part. The history of the Christian church is testimony to the power of God to redeem and transform societies. Based upon God's involvement as demonstrated in past actions and as promised for the present and for the future, the Christian lives truly with hope for society.

The more difficult task, however, is specifying what the Christian hopes for. Some Christians have expected too little of their society. Other Christians have expected the society of which they are a part to be identical with the church. What can

Christians in twentieth century America truly hope for in our
society?

As Christians, we are citizens of this world while at the same
time we are "not of this world" (John 16:11). We live with a
double heritage. This makes difficult a determination of what we
are to hope for. This tension has given rise to several patterns of
hope.[1]

THE MONASTIC PATTERN OF HOPE

The monastic pattern of hope developed early in the history of
the Christian church. It is a tendency similar to that represented
by the Essenes in the time of Jesus. Early believers lived in the
midst of enormous turmoil as they experienced frequent persecution at the hands of pagan governments and heathen religions.
The thirteenth chapter of Revelation describes the believer as
being persecuted by pagan government. The believer experiencing persecution readily identified with this interpretation of
government, and the conclusion was frequently drawn that
governments were inherently evil.

If the believer concludes that government is inherently evil,
the only appropriate response is to withdraw from government. A
tendency has existed throughout the history of the church,
especially in Roman Catholicism, to regard government and
society as being so corrupt that personal purity could only be
attained by entering a monastery or withdrawing to a commune.
The act of withdrawal separated the believer from the corrupt
sphere of society and government by distance, interests, and
commitments.

The monastic tendency eliminates involvement in government
and society for the believer. Society is abandoned to non-Christian
influences, and the believer relinquishes the hope of transforming
and redeeming society. The teachings found in Romans 13 that
government is ordained of God are lost. The Christian who views

government from this perspective has no hope for government.

THE DUALIST PATTERN OF HOPE

The dualist pattern of hope does not advocate withdrawal from society, nor does it have hope for the transformation of society. Society is divided into spiritual and secular realms. Although the believer must live in both, the two do not have much to do with each other. This pattern is similar to the Sadducees of the time of Jesus.

The word which best describes this attitude toward society by believers is passivity. They recognize that God is sovereign and has ordained the political order. But they also regard change and development in the political order as being God's responsibility. Romans 13 is interpreted as meaning that God has ordained government and as having placed in office those who lead government. Since God has established the leaders in office, they are due obedience. They exercise the authority with which God vested them. Opposing them and failing to submit to their authority would be an act of disobedience to God.

Change in government, according to this dualist perspective, will be accomplished by God. The Christian is to pray for the leader. If the leader is evil, the Christian can only pray that God will change the leader or remove him. The only justifiable basis for active opposition to government is when government seeks to compel the believer to violate his own conscience. If the leaders of government seek to compel actions which are forbidden by the Christian faith, such as idolatry, then some form of resistance is justified.

This understanding of the relationship between faith and politics is seen in the Lutheran tradition in Germany. This passive understanding of the Christian's role allowed Adolph Hitler to rise to power and to begin his atrocities without opposition from the church.

Christians may hold this perspective on society for several specific theological reasons. Passivity toward social change may be a result of an emphasis upon the sinfulness of man. It is possible to so emphasize the sinfulness of man that hope for change disappears. This is a type of social pessimism which discounts the possibility of significant change occurring in individuals and societies.

The general understanding of man may also create a passive attitude toward society. At times salvation has been and is portrayed so individualistically that the social nature of man is ignored. When this happens, evangelism and missions can be so oriented toward man's soul that the Hebrew emphasis upon the union of soul and body is ignored. An incomplete understanding of man gives an inadequate view of society.

Another way in which theological emphases may contribute to a dualist perspective of society is through certain eschatological emphases. Some believers become so convinced that the Lord's return is imminent that they imitate the Christians to whom Paul wrote in 2 Thessalonians. When living with an expectation that Jesus will return in the near future, some believers have tended to discount the importance of society. The Lord could return at any moment. No one knows the time except God himself. Believers through the ages have drawn conclusions about the time when Jesus would return. Many systems of interpretation have pointed to specific dates when Jesus would return. He has not yet. We do not know when he will return. We are to live responsibly until he does come. This responsible living involves not only evangelism and missions but also a concern for the social structures of our world, including its government.

THE THEOCRATIC PATTERN OF HOPE

The word *theocracy* describes a form of government found in the life of the people Israel in the Old Testament. God is the supreme king who rules over his people through human agents such as prophets, priests, and kings. In the ideal theocracy envisioned by

God, there would be no king; but God allowed the Israelites to have a king after warning them that human kings were subject to all of the human frailties which ordinary humans experience (1 Sam. 8). God as the divine lawgiver establishes the civil and moral laws which are to guide the nation. All of life was to be lived under the leadership of God. This perspective is similar to the best emphases of the Pharisees in the time of Jesus.

The ideal of a government in which God is the ruler was increasingly distorted as king after king proved inadequate and unworthy to provide the moral and spiritual leadership called for by one who rules as God's representative.

Nothing could be a nobler ideal than establishing this form of government. Unfortunately, in a sinful world, few things have proved more impossible to attain. The theocratic model has been attempted by Christians seeking to make their governments responsive to the intentions of God. One form this has taken is through efforts by the Roman Catholic Church, in different historical periods, to establish a relationship between the Church and the state in which the Church is superior because of its spiritual nature. Since the church is considered by Roman Catholic teaching to be the representative of God in society, the claim is made that Church authorities are justified in acting with the authority of God.

The theocratic pattern has been promoted by some Protestant groups as well. One of the more notable efforts was that of John Calvin in Switzerland. In America, the Puritans sought to establish a theocratic society in New England. More recently some groups in the United States have rekindled this vision.

Passages such as the following are emphasized: "If my people who are called by my name humble themselves, and pray and seek my face, and turn from their wicked ways, then I will hear from heaven and will forgive their sin and heal their land" (2 Chron. 7:14, RSV). To Christians, the new people of God is the church.

The church is the successor to the people of Israel as God's people. The power of the gospel cannot be confined within national or ethnic boundaries. God has grafted the Gentiles into the stump of Jesse. God has raised up children of Abraham from the dust. The gospel is for Jew and Gentile alike.

The teachings of the Bible that God rules nations and acts both as judge and redeemer give hope to the Christian about the world and about society. Because of this assurance, the Christian can hope and work for change. But this does not justify a simple identification of any nation—Israel, the United States, or any other—as God's people. In World War II, Christians in both Germany and the United States were confident that God was on the side of their respective nation, that their nation was God's nation. God's people were in both nations. God's people are scattered among all of the nations of the world. He has ordained government—all government—to promote order, peace, and good behavior. Some governments more fully embody God's desires than others.

Government is ordained of God and exists to serve a function separate from that of the church. Government is the source of power that restrains evildoers and regulates society in nonspiritual matters. Church history abounds with struggles marked by the inability to agree upon a clear delineation between what is spiritual and what is not spiritual. The inevitable result of such a struggle is a bitter conflict over authority and power. Church authorities, motivated by the ideal of establishing God as ruler, become involved in petty strife, selfish ambition, and destructive conflict. In such an environment, both the church and the state fail to fulfill the responsibilities which God has given to them.

THE TRANSFORMING PATTERN OF HOPE

The pattern of hope for society which I accept is the transforming pattern of hope. This understanding is rooted in the prophetic tradition's criticism of the rulers of Israel and in the acceptance by Jesus and the New Testament writers of the limits of government.

Government is one of the institutions established by God. God also established the home and the community of faith, Israel in the Old Testament and the church in the New Testament. God created man to live in the world and to have dominion over it as God's representative, in God's image (Gen. 1:26-27). Great responsibility goes with this role of being in God's image. We are accountable for how we use the opportunities which God has given us. We are answerable to him for our families, our churches, and our government.

If we are responsible to God for the quality of our government, we cannot ignore it or be passive about it. I believe the monastic and dualist patterns of hope for society and government do not take seriously enough the charge to be responsible for the world which God has created. If all Christians followed these patterns, the governments of the world would be abandoned to individuals and groups who embrace some other religious persuasion or espouse no religious belief. This would result in the affairs of government being shaped by values other than Christian values.

Government cannot rise above the sinfulness of man. The prophetic tradition abounds in illustration after illustration of the failure of kings and rulers to abide by God's expectations. Even David, the man after God's own heart, did not succeed in ruling completely as God desired. I believe that the theocratic pattern found throughout the Old Testament was abandoned in the New Testament.[2] In his simple statement about rendering to Caesar and to God that which they are due, Jesus recognized the limitation of government. Man's highest loyalty is to God. It is possible for loyalty to government and loyalty to God to conflict. The government to which limited loyalty was due was the Roman government, a government which served a limited function.

Both Jesus and Paul accepted the Roman government as

legitimate. Neither longed for the days of a theocratic form of government. The government which they accepted was one based on different value systems and different religious beliefs. Certainly the religious pluralism which characterized the Roman Empire was not propagating the gospel or carrying out the task of promoting spirituality. Yet, it was judged as good by Paul because of its restraint of evil and encouragement of good behavior. It was judged as bad by John in Revelation because it had changed from allowing a degree of freedom of conscience to coercing religious idolatry.

Centuries had passed since the full conditions of the theocratic form of government had existed. God is sovereign king and ruler of the nation only when all of the people have accepted his rule. I have surveyed the various stages of theocractic government in the Old Testament in an earlier chapter. In all of the stages, the obedience of the people or the nation was essential. This may be illustrated in several passages. The first chapter of the Book of Joshua records the assumption of leadership by Joshua. He set forth the commands which God had given him for the people. When he finished, the people responded: "And they answered Joshua, 'All that you have commanded us we will do, and wherever you send us we will go. Just as we obeyed Moses in all things, so we will obey you; only may the Lord your God be with you, as he was with Moses!'" (Joshua 1:16-17, RSV). Joshua identified himself as God's chosen leader, proclaimed God's commands to the people, and the leadership of Joshua and God's commands were accepted in obedience by the people. Judges 2 describes a cycle whereby the repentance of the people led to God's selection of a new judge who would be accepted by the people as God's leader.

The theocratic form of government cannot be a model for Christian hope unless the society as a whole has chosen God. Belief in God and obedience to God must be present before the

Old Testament model of government can be considered possible. The New Testament does not set it forth as an ideal. Both Jesus and Paul accepted a different form of government. Efforts throughout history to reestablish a form of theocratic government have failed.

The main reason for the failure of the theocratic pattern of government is the sinfulness of human beings. Sin affects both believers and unbelievers. Because sin affects unbelievers, they would not choose God as the king and the rulers as God's representatives as did the people of Israel under the leadership of Joshua and during the period of the judges. Because sin affects Christians, their efforts at being God's representatives are beset by the same type of problems which David experienced.

Human beings are affected in their decision making, including their political decision making, by their finiteness. Our human limitations produce uncertainties. These uncertainties often require that we make decisions based on general principles which we must apply to some specific issue or question. The Christian has the responsibility of determining, as a free creation of God, how to apply those principles and to find the moral course of action.

The New Testament does not set forth specific laws to guide government and society as the Old Testament did. Since Jesus and the apostles apparently abandoned the concept of a theocratic form of government, such laws were not necessary. The New Testament emphasizes principles and moral values which are relevant for all forms of government. The teachings of Jesus and Paul, with their heavy emphasis upon morality and freedom, are as relevant for a totalitarian society as they are for a democracy.

Paul urged the Christians, "Do not be conformed to this world, but be transformed by the renewal of your mind, that you may prove what is the will of God, what is good and acceptable and perfect" (Rom. 12:2, RSV). This particular passage was not a specific statement about government and the Christian. But it did introduce a section on the ethics of the gospel. Within this larger section (Rom. 12:1 to 15:6) Paul includes his most specific teaching on the Christian and government (Rom. 13:1-7). The world around us is not to be allowed to shape us into its mold. Rather, we are to be agents of transformation. This involves our own selves, the lives of others, and the institutions of society. Government is to be regarded as ordained of God. Like all of life, government is to be transformed. That is a goal of the Christian.

The Christian lives with great hopes. Proclaiming the gospel to all mankind is a part of that hope. The redemption of all mankind is a part of that hope. Transformation of families is a part of that hope. Transformation of the institutions of society—including government—is a part of that hope. Because of hope, the Christian not only sets goals, but also acts.

Several guidelines can be given for the manner in which the Christian seeks to transform society.

First, the Christian seeks the transformation of government by accepting, as Jesus and Paul did, the limited role of government. Government is not expected to promote the gospel. Government is ordained of God and serves his purpose by restraining evil and promoting good. But the promotion of the gospel and responsibility for the spiritual life are not responsibilities of government as in the Old Testament. Even pagan governments can serve the purposes God has ordained them to fulfill. Because the spiritual responsibilities of spreading the gospel and nurturing the spiritual life have been given to the church, government is freed from responsibilities which it cannot perform and thereby enabled to concentrate on more limited responsibilities which it can perform. Because the church is the body of Christ, with many members, the members of Christ's body can penetrate all of society, including government, and transform it.

Second, the Christian recognizes the right of participation in government by individuals who are not Christian. Jesus and Paul lived in a world dominated by the government of pagan Rome. Yet both recognized clearly that this government could function in a manner acceptable to believers. It could provide opportunity for the service of God. It could promote good behavior and punish evil. As believers obeyed and interacted with the government of that day, they were functioning in a pluralist context. The officials of government in the New Testament era were Romans and Jews. The pluralism and diversity of religious belief of that time were not as great as that of the United States in 1983. But it was as great as they could envision in that day. The New Testament era sets the pattern for acceptance of the reality of religious, cultural, and social pluralism in political life.

Third, since the Christian is to be involved in political life and to be involved in transforming it, the Christian will be involved in cooperation with individuals who are not necessarily Christian. Since those individuals may be serving God's purposes for government, Christians should be doing some of the things that they are doing. We are to align ourselves with those who are doing good, regardless of their religious beliefs. We are responsible before God for determination of that which is good. The Bible gives general principles which can guide us in deciding what actions of government would be good and which would be evil. Occasional efforts at the formation of "Christian political parties" have been made. These efforts have failed and are destined to fail. Such groups inevitably become as influenced by the values of their culture as they are by the gospel. No one political position can successfully encompass all that the gospel means for man's social and political life. Modesty requires that Christians be prepared to work and witness alongside others who serve God, although perhaps unknowingly, by their involvement in government.

Fourth, the Christian works and hopes in the political order with the confidence that the Spirit of God is working in that political order. As creator and sustainer, God works to redeem that which he has created and ordained. He has ordained government and works to redeem it and to enable it to fulfill its function. The patriarchs of Israel discovered, much to their dismay, that God was at work in strange places which they had not anticipated, places such as Haran, Egypt, and Gerar. Just as God is not foreign in those lands which appeared strange, he is not remote from political life. His presence may not be apparent. His urgings may not be obeyed. But he is there, waiting for the Christian to join him in the work of redemption.

Fifth, as the Christian acts, he or she is influenced and directed by the moral values of the Christian faith. Many of these values are shared by individuals and groups in a pluralistic culture who operate from a different religious or philosophical perspective than does the Christian. Such values as the sanctity of life, the importance of the family, a desire for peace, and a concern for human equality may be shared by others. Individuals and groups who promote such values are doing the good work of government to which Paul referred. Christians should not press in the political realm values or actions which are embraced only by Christians or for specific theological reasons.

4.
Religious Organizations and Public Policy

Christians in the United States have been involved in politics from the beginning of this nation. Many of the founding fathers were churchmen with strong convictions. In the two centuries which have passed since independence was gained, this involvement has continued, at times more involved than at others. A study of American history can illustrate time and time again the important role Christians have played in the formation, development, and preservation of this nation.

Since this book is primarily oriented toward an analysis of biblical teachings, I will not attempt to present an historical survey of Christian involvement in the public affairs of our nation. Yet I will describe briefly the activities of some organizations which have been formed to give expression to the convictions of different Christian groups.

It is important for the follower of Christ interested in Christian citizenship to have an awareness of these groups. They exist to serve different denominations with varying assignments from those supporting denominations. Yet there is all too frequently a lack of awareness concerning the existence of these groups and of how they function. I think it will be helpful for the Christian to have a certain awareness of these groups. Christians can amplify their impact by working through groups.

It is vital for Christians to be aware of such groups' existence for another reason. Christians are frequently frustrated over the lack of awareness about an existing group which seeks to accomplish the objectives which Christians hope to achieve. New groups are often formed when those same purposes could be achieved by working with an existing group or organization. Heightened awareness of the groups in existence will provide existing alternatives for action in concert with other Christians.

IDENTIFICATION OF GROUPS

The earliest groups seeking to address major social issues were the various abolitionist groups which worked for the elimination of slavery. The next major social issue which moved Christians to organize in groups was the temperance issue. These issues were resolved, at least partially, and other groups have supplanted those that championed those causes.

Albert Menendez wrote an article for *Liberty* magazine which is a helpful guide to the current religious groups which exist to seek to influence politics and social policy.[1] He divides the groups or organizations into several different categories. Although I will use slightly different categories, the article is helpful.

The first category includes the organizations or agencies which are official representatives of specific denominations. Representative agencies which fall into this category are the United States Catholic Conference, the United Methodist Board of Church and Society, the Office of Government Affairs of the Lutheran Council in the U.S.A., the United Presbyterian Washington Office, and the United Church of Christ Office for Church in Society. The Southern Baptist Convention has established the Christian Life Commission which works in the field of applied Christianity. The Convention also cooperates with other Baptist conventions through the Baptist Joint Committee, which works in the field of religious liberty.

While most of these groups operate broadly in the overall field of social policy, some of them deal more specifically with concerns for peace. This is true of agencies maintained by three of the historic "peace" churches: The Church of the Brethren Washington Office, the Mennonite Central Committee, and the Friends Committee on National Legislation.

Catholic and Jewish influence is also expressed through groups: Catholic influence largely through the United States Catholic Conference, Jewish influence through a number of organizations, including the American Jewish Committee, the American Jewish Congress, and the National Conference on Christians and Jews.

The single-issue organizations are a second category. There are several major organizations which assume some position on the abortion issue. Two of these, the Religious Coalition for Abortion Rights and Catholics for a Free Choice, support some measure of freedom of choice in abortion matters. Two others, the National Committee for Human Life Amendment, Inc., and the Christian Action Council, advocate more restrictive positions on the abortion issue.

Several organizations act with single-issue concern in the field of church-state relations. The oldest and most prominent is Americans United for the Separation of Church and State. Founded as Protestants and Other Americans United for the Separation of Church and State, the organization has broadened its organizational base. It has worked extensively to oppose government aid to parochial schools. Citizens for Educational Freedom is a predominantly Roman Catholic group which supports govenment aid for parochial schools.

A third category of organizations consists of umbrella organizations, those which have varied memberships of either denominations or organizations. The traditional umbrella organizations are those such as the National Council of Churches and the National Association of Evangelicals. The former organization is composed of denominations which tend to be referred to as "mainline" churches, while the former is composed of churches which have been identified more traditionally as "evangelical" or conservative. I think it is more accurate to designate the constituency of the National Association of Evangelicals as being some of the fundamentalist denominations within the United States.

A different set of umbrella organizations is comprised by those which constitute the New Religious Right. They differ from the other umbrella organizations in several points. First, they are umbrella organizations in the sense that they have members who represent a wide variety of religious backgrounds. Rather than having member denominations, they have members who are individuals. Second, these organizations tend to be centered more in the work of a particular personality. Third, these organizations have been built by reliance on some form of communication technology, principally television and computers.

A number of organizations and individuals should be mentioned. The first organization is the Committee for the Survival of a Free Congress. The principal figure behind this organization is Paul Weyrich. John T. Tolan is the major figure behind the National Conservative Political Action Committee, which has generated substantial sums of money for conservative political candidates. A third organization is the Conservative Caucus, headed by Howard Phillips. A fourth is Christian Voice, with Gary Jarmin as the principal spokesman. A fifth is the Round Table, headed by Ed McAteer. The sixth, and perhaps most widely known, is Moral Majority, organized and headed by Jerry Falwell.

Pat Robertson has no special organization, but his influence is seen in his television program, "The 700 Club." Richard Viguerie, publisher of *Conservative Digest*, is a computer genius who is closely associated with a number of the organizations and their leaders.

These organizations represent a mixture of conservative economic and political philosophies and traditional moral concerns.

For example, the Moral Majority agenda includes a commitment to four specific moral concerns: pro-family, pro-life, pro-morality, and pro-America. From these commitments, strong opposition has been directed against abortion, the Equal Rights Amendment, pornography, and crime, while strong support has been voiced for Israel and for increased military spending.

Paul Weber is one of the few individuals to study religious agencies seeking to influence public policy. He drew a number of conclusions in a recent study.[2] Some of them are a little surprising. The religious agencies or organizations are almost evenly divided into liberal and conservative classifications. The 1970s were a time of enormous growth in involvement of conservative religious organizations. Almost 70 percent of the forty new groups established were conservative in their orientation, according to Weber.

Almost half of the seventy-four groups are classified by Weber as single-issue groups. The others work with a wide range of social issues. The groups identified as conservative in their political and religious concerns are much more likely to be single-issue groups.

HOW THESE GROUPS FUNCTION

The number of groups which try to influence public policy is substantial. Some years ago I set out to understand these groups better and sent a questionnaire to over forty of them. I received about fifteen responses. The groups responding were Protestant agencies representing most of the major denominations. From these responses I was able to draw some conclusions about how these groups functioned and what methods they used. The study was helpful for me in understanding the groups because little had been written about them. My study was influenced by an older work, by Eugene Ebersole, which is still an informative, though dated, treatment of the functioning of these groups.[3]

The agencies studied described their work primarily as educational and informative. At other times their activities were designed to influence the political process, either directly or indirectly.

Three methods of engaging in political education and providing information were being used. They were legislative analysis, compilation of congressional voting records, and political education through more generalized approaches.

All but two of the agencies studied engaged in some general analysis of legislation. Only three of the agencies attempted to compile congressional voting records.

One of the surprising results of the study was the relatively small amount of time and effort given to political education. Most of the agencies relied upon national and regional seminars for their main thrust in political education. Staff members of the various agencies were heavily involved in speaking engagements.

Political education had as its objective the mobilization of a constituency. Information was provided so that groups reached by that information would act and would influence the political process.

The groups studied engaged in actions which went beyond political education. They sought to influence government through their own actions. They engaged in different kinds of action. They spent varying amounts of time doing it, but most of the groups sought to do more than educate.

The use of *indirect techniques* of influencing government was generally accepted as valid and practiced. Some of the agencies contacted influential supporters and asked them to express specific opinions to their congressmen. Others were hesitant to employ such specific action. They depended solely on spontaneous responses from supporters or the public to their information and education.

Several *direct techniques* of influencing government were noted.

Some of the groups have sought to influence the platforms of the political parties; several of the groups had testified before platform committees.

A second direct technique, influencing nominations and elections, was seldom used and with very little effectiveness. Perhaps the most successful illustration of this direct technique to date is the role of the New Religious Right in several of the 1980 elections.

A third type of direct influence was the cultivating of congressmen sympathetic to the interests of the group. Although only six groups indicated their involvement in such activity, perhaps this was the most successful direct effort at influencing government. In recent years, this approach has increased significantly.

A fourth direct technique was appearance before congressional committees to provide information and to express viewpoints. Such a technique was accepted as valid, although not widely employed. Although no statistics are readily available, I believe this technique of direct influence has increased considerably in recent years.

The groups or agencies have generally become more active in the years since I conducted my earlier study. I think there are several reasons for this. First, there is less reluctance to avoid activity which might be classified as lobbying. We now more readily accept lobbying activity as not only legitimate, but even necessary. The Christian groups which seek to influence government generally use their influence for nonsectarian, general welfare purposes. Second, there is less fear today than ten years ago about challenges to tax-exempt status.

But a third reason is even more important. Social problems have increased in complexity. There is tremendous concern about moral decay in society. In such an environment, the gospel demands that Christians seek to bring influence to bear on society.

The range of issues which has concerned these agencies is extremely wide. Until recent years, most of the issues have involved advocacy for some cause benefiting the general welfare. This advocacy might be primarily for the benefit of a specific group such as the support of civil rights causes. It might be for a broader segment of society, as with support for federal aid to public education.

Most of the religious groups active in government have focused on general welfare concerns. They sought to support social values held by a diversity of religious traditions. This was seen in the support of the civil rights movement of the 1950s and 1960s and the opposition to war in the 1960s and early 1970s.

Something different is happening. Organizations are more active than ever before in support of specific sectarian causes and sectarian beliefs. Support has increased immensely for such sectarian causes as government support of prayer in the public schools and tuition tax credits. Specific theological beliefs are at the heart of opposition to abortion and of support for a military buildup, especially in support of Israel.

Perhaps the most dramatic change in this area within recent years has been the emergence of New Religious Right organizations.

5.
The Separation of Church and State

The greatest contribution the United States has made to religion is the concept of religious liberty and its corollary, the separation of church and state. Those of us who have been raised in this cradle of religious liberty take this precious freedom all too lightly. Any attempt to understand the role of religious faith in political involvement must take seriously the heritage carved out by our ancestors.

The early settlers of the United States were raised in European nations which had established churches. Established churches were churches which were recognized as official arms of the state, were given special places of authority, and were supported by tax money. The Lutheran Church was the established church of Germany. The Anglican Church was the established church of England. The Roman Catholic Church was the established church of Spain. Throughout Europe, this pattern dominated.

This practice of having an established church simply followed an historical pattern seen in most nations. Most major religions originated in a national setting where the religions became so enmeshed with the culture that the two became inseparable. Historically, one who was a native of India was a Hindu. Japanese were Shinto or Buddhist, or both. Chinese were Confucian or Taoist. For unnumbered centuries, limited exposure to other cultures and religious faiths prevented the vast majority of individuals from being aware that other religious beliefs were alternatives. Group pressures and national cultures exerted strong influences prohibiting persons who were aware of other religious faiths from renouncing the national faith and choosing another.

The early settlers of the United States came from several different religious traditions. The New England settlers came from the Puritan tradition stemming from the influence of John Calvin. Congregationalism was the dominant church in that region. Roger Williams was an outcast because of his dissent against the establishment of Congregationalism. Virginia was dominated by the Church of England, which became the Episcopal Church in America. Maryland was dominated by Roman Catholic influence. Throughout the colonies, a number of churches were dominant. A number of states recognized one church as the official church of that state. But four states—Rhode Island, Pennsylvania, Delaware, and New Jersey—never had established churches. By the time of the Revolutionary War, religious dissent even in those states which had established churches had grown. Of the states which did have established churches, most of them had severed the official tie with the established church long before Massachusetts did in 1833, making the United States completely free from any form of establishment of religion. The practice of religious liberty, fought for by so many, was at last formally guaranteed by the states.[1]

RELIGIOUS LIBERTY AND THE FIRST AMENDMENT

One of the debates which occurs with frequency regards the intentions of the founding fathers with respect to the role of Christianity in the affairs of government. The debate is testimony to the desire of a religious people to establish religious liberty.

The debate about government's attitude toward Christianity is complicated by the absence of a concise, clear delineation of the concept of separation of church and state. One thing which the concept clearly does not mean is that citizens involved in government are to refrain from talking about God. Government officials are free to discuss their religious beliefs in both private and public. This is so common that the public has become accustomed to such expressions of religious piety. This is especially true for government officials who are Christians or Jews. Our coins bear the phrase, "In God we trust." The pledge of allegiance to the flag contains the phrase "one Nation under God." We are a religious people and signs of religiosity adorn our political system.

It is no surprise that our government manifests these signs of religious belief, for most of the founding fathers were religious. They were Baptists, Episcopalians, Congregationalists, Methodists, Quakers, Roman Catholics, and Deists. Most of them embraced some religious orientation. And yet they adopted a constitution which sought to assure religious freedom while prohibiting the federal government from establishing a particular religion or church.

Thomas Jefferson, a Deist, was the most influential person in the formation of the Constitution and its Bill of Rights. By following some of Jefferson's actions and statements, we can gain a glimpse of the intentions of the founding fathers.

Jefferson was a resident of Virginia. Virginia had established the Episcopal Church as its official church. Perhaps the first step in the direction of religious toleration was the recognition of dissenting clergy (clergy who were other than Episcopal) as chaplains during the Revolutionary War. Several steps were necessary to provide not only freedom of opportunity for dissenting groups but also freedom from financial support of the Episcopal Church through taxation. But once these were attained in 1786, only the remnant of establishment remained until it also was abolished in 1802.

Jefferson's autobiography provides important insight into the adoption of the "Statute of Virginia for Religious Liberty" in 1786.

> Where the preamble declares that coercion is a departure from the plan of the holy author of our religion, an amendment was proposed, by inserting the words, "Jesus Christ," so that it should read, "a departure from the plan of Jesus Christ, the holy author of our religion"; the insertion was rejected by a great majority, in proof that they meant to comprehend, within the mantle of its protection, the Jew and the Gentile, the Christian and the Mahometan, the Hindoo, the infidel of every denomination.[2]

The statement reflects that most individuals of his day were religious. But it avoided specifically the attempt to make the statement a Christian statement. Religious liberty under the Virginia statute was not based upon any specific recognition of Christianity, Judaism, or any other religion. Religious men sought to provide freedom for even the infidel. They avoided any religious establishment which would infringe upon the infidel as well as the believer.

This same Thomas Jefferson, who wrote The Declaration of Independence, was one of the main drafters of the Constitution of the United States. The Constitutional Convention brought together a broad cross section of individuals, representing most of the major religious groups. The only section of the Constitution which related to religion was Article VI, which contained a provision providing that no religious test should be required for an office held under the United States government. All evidence suggests that the principles of religious toleration and nonestablishment were so widely accepted as a necessity that they were not even discussed. Some thought the issue might be open to question. Shortly after the ratification of the Constitution, a movement was begun to make even more specific the principle of religious freedom, with the result that the Bill of Rights was adopted in 1791.

The First Amendment provides that religious freedom is a right of all citizens and that there shall be no establishment of religion by the federal government. No individual shall be required to pay taxes to support the religious activity of any group. Connected with the religious freedom guarantee of the First Amendment are the rights of free speech, free press, the right of free assembly, and the right to petition government for redress. To the religious person, these other guarantees make explicit the fullness of religious freedom, assuring that the right is not speculative and abstract, but one which can find expression and protection.

The history of the United States reflects numerous efforts at modifying the position of the founding fathers that not only should no denomination be established but that Christianity not be recognized as an official religion. These repeated efforts are not surprising, given the fact that the American people are in general a religious people. Also, Christianity has had a profound influence on the formation of our society and its culture. These efforts are causes for concern because they illustrate the difficulty of firmly preserving the principle of religious liberty.

This brief survey describes the perspective on church and state which I feel represents most adequately our nation's heritage of religious freedom. This perspective will be demonstrated by examining some of the contemporary problems dealing with church and state relations.

CURRENT ISSUES RELATED TO CHURCH-STATE SEPARATION

In application of the principle of separation, a number of problem areas have developed.

The problem of definition of religion and church. Church-state issues are no longer as simple as they were when the only religions to be considered were Christianity (both Protestant and Catholic) and Judaism. The twentieth century is a period of religious proliferation of several sorts. First, there has been a tremendous growth in the influence of Oriental religions. Second, numerous "new religions" have emerged and developed in recent decades. Third, the courts have recognized nontheistic religions as deserving of protection, as in the case of a conscientious objector who objects to war for legitimate moral reasons.

The First Amendment of the United States Constitution prohibits the establishment of any religion and guarantees the free exercise of religion. Ruling on establishment and free exercise cases requires the courts at times to decide whether or not a claim offered by a group is in fact a religious claim. This has been made more difficult, not only by the proliferation of different types of religions, but also by growth in the number of individuals and groups which seek to exploit the free exercise status for ulterior motives, such as tax exemption.

In addition, various federal and state statutes refer to religion and churches. Application of these statutes requires some determination as to what constitutes a religion or a church. These determinations, while assisted by precedents from First Amendment cases, nonetheless require some additional determination because the courts have tried to avoid defining what religion is and what a church is.

Government actions which threaten separation. Interference by the government in the concerns of religious organizations is a growing area of tension. Most people recognize that even the rights secured by the First Amendment are not absolute in the extent of their exercise. The freedom of speech does not justify an individual who shouts "fire" in a crowded theater. The freedom of religion does not allow an individual or group to practice human sacrifice. Freedom of the press does not allow a newspaper to blatantly tell lies and fabricate untruths about an individual. These rights are held to be subject to governance and restraint as the individual rights are balanced against the rights of society. Society through its government exercises legitimate regulation of these rights.

One of the ongoing areas of debate is the matter of *tax exemption* of religious organizations. Traditionally, religious organizations have sought and been granted the status of tax exemption. This has been justified because of the power implicit in taxation to control the group or individual taxed. There is frequent criticism of this policy. Churches have used on occasions their status to engage in business activities which conflict with private businesses which pay taxes. This created a favorable position for the businesses owned or controlled by churches. Pressures have mounted to halt these practices and to require that businesses owned by churches be subject to taxation since these businesses have nothing to do with the place of worship. As a part of this growing concern over the fiscal responsibility of the church, many observers are calling upon the churches to pay for civil services— such as fire protection and law enforcement—from which they benefit with the rest of society. Churches may anticipate a growing trend calling for taxation of all facilities not being used for worship or education. Such a trend will not affect the place of ministry, but will limit the degree to which the churches can own other property without taxation.

Another action of the government which is of concern at the present is *regulation* of the type carried out by the Equal Employment Opportunity Commission (EEOC). Our government has sought to assure the civil rights of individuals in the areas of sex, religion, and race. Our government through legislation has sought to prohibit discrimination on these bases. As a part of this regulation, a controversy has developed about the extent to which the government can regulate the actions of institutions connected with churches, usually institutions such as colleges and private schools.

A court case which will have considerable impact in coming years is the action by the EEOC against Southwestern Baptist Theological Seminary. The EEOC sought information about employment practices of the seminary. The seminary refused on the grounds that it was an integral mission of the church and that the EEOC would be excessively entangling itself in the operation of the seminary to require such information. On appeal, the seminary was upheld in its contention that it should not have to submit employment information regarding administrative, instructional, and ministerial positions. But the Court of Appeals ruled that it did have to submit information on other jobs. The Supreme Court upheld these conclusions.

The freedom of religion requires restraint upon the part of government to avoid encroaching upon these functions of the church which are uniquely religious in nature. We can anticipate more conflict in the days ahead as the courts seek a balance between the right of freedom of religion and the duty of governmental regulation. Christians and other religious people will be watching this area of tension with much interest. Some insight into the future resolution of this tension will be given when the Supreme Court of the United States rules on the tax exempt status of Bob Jones University, a college which practices certain policies which discriminate racially for religious reasons. This case should be decided in the 1982-83 session of the court.

Positions of religious groups which threaten separation. Frequently tension in the separation of church and state results from actions by religious groups or individuals. These involve pressures for inclusion of religious activities in public institutions or for various forms of financial aid.

One of the most frequent areas of pressure for change is in the area of *school prayer*. The practice of having state-sponsored prayers was forbidden in 1962 and devotional readings of the Bible in 1963. These practices were occurring in about two percent of the school districts of the United States at the time. They were taking place in the classroom, under the supervision of teachers or other school personnel. As such, they were judged not to be voluntary. Since the students were in the classrooms in response to state law and attendance was required, these actions were considered to be sponsored by the state. Students were thus considered to be required to participate in these devotional exercises. Thus, their "participation" was considered to be compulsory.

Attempts have been made frequently to pass a constitutional amendment which would allow policies such as those prohibited by the Supreme Court in 1962 and 1963. They seek to amend the Constitution to make voluntary prayer possible again. They cite public opinion polls which frequently claim that 60 to 70 percent of the citizens want such an amendment. Usually those who press for such an amendment are Christians who hold the position that the United States is a "Christian nation." They believe that our forefathers would not have intended that the type of prayer they call "voluntary prayer" be disallowed.

A current effort at a voluntary prayer amendment is being championed by many conservative Christians. President Ronald Reagan has endorsed such an amendment, Senator Jesse Helms of North Carolina is a strong advocate of this amendment. He was asked a series of questions seeking to determine the meaning of the practice he called voluntary prayer. Would he find acceptable as voluntary prayer the practice of a third grade teacher writing the words of the "Hail Mary" on the board and inviting the students to join in reciting the words? As a Baptist, the Senator answered that he would find this practice acceptable. He thought that individuals of other religious persuasions also would. One of his contentions was that no children had been hurt by such school prayer.

Opponents of the school prayer amendments contend that such an amendment is neither religiously wise nor constitutionally consistent. At one time or another, such an amendment has been opposed by virtually every major religious body in the United States. Opposition has been based on several objections. The first is that it is a violation of religious liberty to subject children to state-sponsored or state-supported prayers which may be inconsistent with their own religious faith. Prayer under the supervision of a school official is state-supported prayer. Another objection is that the amendment would put the government into the business of officially sanctioning prayers and determining which ones are nondenominational enough to be used and allowed. Also, they emphasize that truly voluntary prayer has not been prohibited. Therefore, no need exists for an amendment. I agree with this position.

Prayer is too important to all religious persons to be trivialized by state-authored prayer which is so nonsectarian as to be offensive to Protestant, Catholic, Jewish, and other religious bodies. Prayer involves some specificity of religious belief. The Christian approaches the act of prayer differently than does the Muslim or the Buddhist. The distinctiveness of this difference should not be lost through well-meaning efforts at making the public schools more religious than they should be.

A second pressure exerted by religious groups upon government is the pressure for some form of *religious teaching in the public school*. The Supreme Court has prohibited the devotional reading of the Bible and other religious literature. The reading of religious books for literary and historical purposes has not been prohibited. They may be read when religion is being studied as an historical phenomenon, as a part of the school curriculum.

Some of these efforts have involved attempts to have "creation science" recognized as scientific theory, not as religious literature. As yet, this effort has not succeeded in convincing governmental structures that the foundation is scientific rather than religious. A similar result occurred when advocates of Transcendental Meditation attempted to convince school authorities and the courts that Transcendental Meditation was scientific rather than religious. The courts determined that it was a manifestation of Oriental religion and only indirectly, if at all, a science.

A third source of pressure from religious groups is the pressure for financial aid. The main form this takes at present is pressure for *tuition tax credits*. If implemented, this would allow parents of children attending private schools to deduct part or all of the tuition in the form of a tax credit.

The proponents of tuition tax credits proceed on the theory that the benefit is to the parent and not to the religious institution. They contend that the parents who elect to send their children to private schools are being penalized by having to pay taxes to support public schools and to pay tuition to educate their own children. They argue that tax credits are an equitable means of partially avoiding financial support of two school systems. Most of the private schools which would benefit are schools with some religious affiliation. The parents who would benefit from the tuition tax credits would thereby be enabled to practice wider freedom of choice related to their children's education. Formerly this position was championed by the Roman Catholic Church. Now it is being championed by conservative and fundamentalist Christians who are withdrawing their children from public schools. Some support comes from private schools established for segregationist purposes. Certainly I do not intend to suggest that most of the support for tuition tax credits is coming from segregationist motives and institutions.

Opponents of tuition tax credits contend that the primary

effect of this type of legislation is to advance religious institutions which exist to serve sectarian purposes. The rationale offered for attending most of these schools is a religious rationale. Churches which establish schools at least usually have religious purposes which they hope to serve. The test of financial aid, under both institutional and child-benefit theories, is whether or not the primary result is to advance religion. If that is the primary effect, the proposed aid is considered unconstitutional. Otherwise, the aid would be offered to religious institutions with money derived from taxing individuals who did not embrace that religious persuasion.

Some types of aid to religious institutions are acceptable because they do not support the religious functions of church schools or students attending religious institutions. This aid is usually indirect. A school system may provide bus transportation to students enrolled in parochial schools. Some colleges have used construction grants to build buildings which are not used for religious instruction, buildings such as libraries.

The founding fathers were wise in seeking to prevent debate over the use of funds for religious institutions from becoming a major disturbance. The number of plans which have been devised to try to get around the Constitution is astonishing. The more that church institutions secure and become dependent upon government funds and policies, the more entangled church and government will become. When entanglement of an institutional nature occurs, freedoms are lost. For the Christian, penetration of the political order is different from entanglement with it.

6.
The Dangers of Civil Religion

One of the greatest dangers, both to government and to authentic religion, is civil religion. Civil religion is a mixture of religion and politics which serves the interests of the state. In civil religion, the religious institutions are used as means of generating support for political positions. Approval is sought from religious leaders for actions of the state. The religious institutions assume a secondary role of importance in supporting the actions of political leaders.

Civil religion is the result of political domination and manipulation of religious institutions. When religious institutions dominate, the political institutions of a society wind up supporting religious causes. The relationship between the Roman Catholic Church and the state in the Middle Ages illustrates what happens when religious institutions dominate. The concept of civil religion is nonetheless a difficult one to communicate. I want to use a slightly different approach in describing civil religion than followed by many who have written on the subject. I also want to use some familiar biblical illustrations to demonstrate how civil religion functioned in the events of the Bible. I think the use of these familiar stories will assist in understanding how governments frequently use religion. After looking at these, perhaps it will be easier to understand some of the characteristics of civil religion which I will describe.

CIVIL RELIGION IN THE BIBLE

It is possible to find many illustrations of civil religion in the Bible. I think that it would be helpful to focus upon civil religion not only in the people of Israel, but also in several of the nations with which they had contact. Even within Israel, it is possible to see how civil religion functions in different times and ways.

CIVIL RELIGION IN EGYPT AND IN ROME

Perhaps one of the most familiar stories in the Old Testament is the story of Moses and the Exodus. The children of Israel were in slavery in the land of *Egypt*. God had delivered the descendants of Jacob through the success of Joseph in Egypt. God had prepared a way for the children of Jacob to escape the famine in the land of Palestine by going to the land of Egypt, where Joseph had prepared storehouses of food.

But a new generation had arisen, a generation which knew not Joseph. New rulers governed the land of Egypt. These rulers pursued policies of oppression which made the plight of the children of Israel unbearable. God selected Moses as the one who would deliver the children of Israel from this bondage. The story of the call of Moses, his reluctance to assume the responsibility God gave him, and his eventual obedience is well known.

Egypt had a form of government which recognized a single male as the supreme authority. This individual was known as the pharaoh. Usually the pharaoh was the descendant of the previous ruling authority and succeeded to the position of authority at the death of his father. At times there were changes that occurred through turmoil, violence, and rebellion.

The pharaoh was recognized as divine by the Egyptians. The Egyptian religion was polytheistic, espousing and practicing belief in many gods. The chief god in the Egyptian religion was Ra, the sun god. The pharaoh was recognized as divine and was considered to be a representation of the sun god. As such, he was to rule with complete authority. His role as ruler was supported by a wide variety of religious leaders. Some of them were magicians. Some of them were wise men and teachers. The end result was that Egyptian government was among the most religious to be found in world history.

The story of the Exodus and the life of Moses is found in the Book of Exodus. The story of Moses recounts the plagues and the conflicts with the Egyptian authorities. Moses had frequent contact with Pharaoh throughout this time. One of the most illustrative statements of Pharaoh occurs in the first conversation with Moses. After Moses repeats to Pharaoh the words of the Lord, Pharaoh responds by saying, "Who is the Lord, that I should heed his voice and let Israel go? I do not know the Lord, and moreover I will not let Israel go" (Ex. 5:2, RSV). These words betray a deeper meaning than might appear on the surface. Pharaoh was not simply confessing an ignorance of the Lord. He was focusing upon the fact that he himself was divine and that he was the one who was in control in the land of Egypt. He was affronted that a foreigner would come into his own palace and pass communication from a foreign deity to the very one who was considered in control of all Egypt.

Pharaoh considered his role as ruler to be without qualification. He considered himself to rule absolutely. He considered himself to be answerable to no one in his role as ruler. His understanding of his role as ruler predates the concept of the "divine right of kings" which appears later in European history. If the ruler is absolute, answerable to no one, then anyone who challenges the ruler is not only challenging a political policy, but also a religious belief.

Pharaoh's response was to punish not only Moses, but also the people of Israel. One way of punishing Moses was increasing the burden borne by the other Israelites so that they would blame Moses for their plight. Pharaoh did this. In so doing, he

embarked upon a policy of resisting God's intentions for the
children of Israel. He did this not only for political reasons, but
also for religious reasons. He would not allow his religious
authority to be challenged any more than his political authority.

The story of the plagues begins to unfold. This story is best
understood as a great religious controversy between the gods of
Egypt and the Lord who had spoken to Moses. Different miracles
were performed. Several miracles were performed also by the
Egyptians (Ex. 7:22; 8:7). Among the religious figures who
supported the religion of Egypt were the magicians who served
Pharaoh. These figures can be contrasted with the prophets of the
Old Testament very easily. Whereas the true prophet in the Old
Testament spoke the word of God frequently in judgment against
the political leaders, the Egyptian wise men used their magic in
unqualified support of Pharaoh.

But even the magicians were unable to serve Pharaoh in the
way which he desired. Although they duplicated some of the
plagues which God performed upon the Egyptians through
Moses, they soon exhausted their capacities. After being unable
to deal with the gnats, the magicians said, "This is the finger of
God" (Ex. 8:19, RSV). Even the magicians concluded that they
were unable to deliver for Pharaoh that which he desired.

The rest of the story of Moses and Pharaoh is an unfolding of
the manner in which a political ruler ignored all evidence because
of his religious dogmatism. Pharaoh, from a political perspective,
concluded that he was unable to control the situation with the
Israelites on a number of occasions. But he constantly became
stubborn and dogmatic because of his religious confidence. He
ignored the events at hand because of his desire to remain
unchallenged in his leadership in Egypt. His religious beliefs
about himself encouraged him to hold out and to be confident
that Egypt would be victorious again. The rest of the story, which
is so well known, demonstrates the inadequacy of the Egyptian

religion to delivery that which it promised.

The Egyptian religion was a religion which existed to support the political aspirations of the nation of Egypt in general and of the ruling authorities in particular. They wanted to remain supreme and unchallenged in their leadership. When they failed to deal with a foreign enemy, it suggested that they were unable to deal as effectively as political rulers as they promised. Weak rulers did not live long in a barbaric time. They used the religious beliefs of the people to sustain their leadership and to command obedience from the people. This worked well most of the time.

The civil religion of *Rome* was remarkably similar to the civil religion of Egypt. The thirteenth chapter of Revelation describes some of the functioning of the Roman government and its utilization of religion to accomplish its objectives. The Book of Revelation was written at a time later than the life of the apostle Paul. Roman government had become more hostile to Christianity and was actively persecuting it. The perspective on the Roman government found in Revelation 13 differs from that found in Romans 13.

It is important to see more clearly the manner in which the Roman government used religion to accomplish its purposes. The Roman government sought to be supreme and to command unqualified allegiance. The service and worship of Rome consisted in saying, "Who is like the beast, and who can fight against it?" (Rev. 13:4, RSV). The idolatry of Rome was twofold. First, it advocated the worship of other gods than the Lord. Secondly, it asserted its own supremacy. It deified itself. We understand today more fully that a god does not have to be simply a supreme being. A god can be something which is given unqualified allegiance and obedience. A god can be a nation, a life-style, or an ideology. Whatever a person is willing to recognize as supreme and determinative for his or her life's purpose becomes, in fact, the god of that person. Rome sought to be the god which was in fact due unqualified allegiance. In seeking to be that, it found useful the advancement of religions which would support Rome as supreme.

In the latter half of Revelation 13, beginning with verse 11, is a description of the religious institutions which served Rome. In the first half of the chapter, the blasphemous activity of Rome is described in general. Now the religious institutions are identified as being agents of that blasphemy. The religious institutions have the authority of Rome. The religious institutions seek to compel individuals to worship Rome, specifically the gods officially recognized by Rome, especially Caesar. The religious institutions and religious leaders sought to use signs and wonders to convince people of the power and of the greatness of Rome. Religious institutions engaged in deceit in perpetuating the power of Rome and in bidding people to serve Rome. The religious institutions sought to institute policies that would coerce individuals to worship and to serve Rome in order to participate as citizens.

Rome needed these religious institutions, and these religious institutions needed Rome. Humans are frequently subject to superstition. It might be argued that human beings living in the time of Rome, who were less educated than modern man, were more superstitious. A study of that time certainly indicates that a wide variety of religions existed and preyed upon the superstitions of people of that day. Humans frequently can be convinced to do something for reasons of superstition when they would not do similar things for reasons of loyalty. Superstition can create fear. Fear can move individuals to do things which they would ordinarily refuse to do. Fear of the unknown, fear of eternal punishment, fear of punishment of loved ones; these fears often are more powerful than the fear of direct, physical punishment. Rome understood that religion could motivate people, through superstition, fear, and signs, to be obedient and to serve the political goals which it sought to accomplish.

The religious institutions needed Rome. These religious institutions found protection and benefit from being a part of the official system of government. They were wed to the purposes of the state of Rome. It was to their advantage as individuals and institutions to be looked upon with signs of favor and to receive the benefits Rome gave to those who served it well. One is mindful of the similarity between this and the Pharisees in the time of the New Testament. There is similarity between this and the false prophets in the nation of Israel in the Old Testament. When religious individuals and religious institutions define their purposes by the service to be rendered to the nation, civil religion is both present and degrading in its impact.

It is difficult to speculate upon the motives of the religious leaders who served Rome. Perhaps they were sincere. Perhaps they were not. Where religious liberty is not possible, even individuals who begin with good motives become susceptible to greed, ambition, and manipulation. Such seems clearly to be the case with the religion of Rome.

JEWISH SYNCRETISM AND CIVIL RELIGION

The Jewish people, throughout their history, lived with the tendency and temptation toward religious syncretism, mixing the worship of the Lord with that of other deities. The Jewish people lived in a land surrounded by foreign nations which worshiped deities other than the Lord. The Egyptian people worshiped the sun, the river, and many animals of nature. The people of Canaan worshiped fertility deities. Through this frequent contact with Egyptians, Canaanites, and others of the ancient Near East, the people of Israel were constantly tempted to practice syncretism.

Many illustrations of syncretism and civil religion could be given. I have chosen to focus upon two of these. The first involves the life of King Solomon and the second involves the conflict between Elijah and the prophets of Baal.

King Solomon was perhaps one of the most fortunate men who has ever lived. He had the privilege of having for his father King David, who was described as being a man after God's own heart. He had the opportunity of benefiting from the success David had accomplished. David secured peace for the nation, extended the boundaries of the land, and secured the land from its enemies. Solomon had the opportunity of becoming king at a time when no great battles had to be fought, when peace existed in the land, and when economic prosperity could be achieved rather easily. He had an opportunity and a legacy which few men in history have ever had.

Solomon's beginning as king is widely recognized as promising. The story of his prayer for wisdom is detailed in 1 Kings 3. He pleased God by his prayer for wisdom. He was privileged to build the Temple which his father had desired to build. History has been kind to Solomon. His good deeds are possibly remembered far more clearly than his weaknesses. He is generally regarded as a strong king. He was not without fault. He seems to have been materialistic in his political goals. He used forced labor in the construction of the buildings which he erected.

One of the flaws of Solomon which is remembered frequently is connected with his many marriages. Jokes are often made about the ambition of even a king having so many wives. I find that the jokes often detract from a clearer reading of the meaning of 1 Kings 11 where Solomon's greatest weakness is described. Throughout the early part of that chapter, the practice of religious syncretism is described. The religious syncretism perhaps originated and grew because of Solomon's practice of having many wives, but it represented his lack of commitment and control.

One of the ways in which Solomon sought to maintain peace was through marital alliances with other rulers. A marriage with the daughter of a ruler of another nation or people would be the occasion for a treaty that would govern affairs of state, commerce, and peace. Through these practices, peace was supposedly secured, extended, and preserved. Solomon practiced this kind of foreign policy far more extensively than any other king of Israel. The results of this practice were very mixed. He secured his political goals at the expense of the very heart of the covenant faith.

Solomon in marrying the foreign women was entering into marital relations with women who were not of the covenant faith of the Lord. He not only tolerated the worship of other gods, but also participated with his wives in that worship. The prohibition against marriage with other nations was a religious prohibition. The psychology of interpersonal relationships is such that the religion of one person will influence the other. To Solomon's shame, his wives influenced him far more extensively in matters of religious faith than he influenced them. In 1 Kings 11:3, we are told that Solomon was swayed by his wives in his religious belief. He is described as following Ashtoreth, Milcom, and Chemosh. These deities represent rivals of the Lord. They are deities of nations who were Israel's historic enemies. For some of them, child sacrifice was practiced. Solomon even built places of worship for them. One of the saddest judgments that can be pronounced on a king is pronounced upon Solomon with the statement, "And so he did for all his foreign wives, who burned incense and sacrificed to their gods" (1 Kings 11:8, RSV).

Careful reading of this chapter exposes Solomon as one of the most dramatic practitioners of civil religion. For Solomon, political objectives appear to have dominated religious concerns. To accomplish his political objectives he engaged in the practice of marrying foreign wives, in violation of religious prohibition. To deal domestically with his foreign wives, he found it necessary and helpful to not only tolerate their religious practices, but also to participate and to build places of worship for them. The city of Jerusalem, the city of God, the city captured by David for the capital of Israel, thus became a city literally teeming with places of worship for Solomon's wives. The religion of his wives not only furthered their role in Solomon's political objectives, but also distorted his faith and detracted him from following in the path of his father, David. Perhaps no sadder illustration of the influence of civil religion can be found. The king who prayed for wisdom lived with foolishness.

The next illustration of the tragedy of civil religion can be found in the story of Elijah. Elijah stood as God's representative in opposing the civil religion being practiced in his day. One of the tendencies which recurred throughout the history of Israel was to worship Baal, the fertility deity worshiped by the Canaanites. The land of Canaan was an agricultural land. It sustained its livelihood from crops and cattle. The success or the failure of the economy of Canaan depended upon the fertility of the cattle and crops. The Canaanites had for centuries worshiped Baal and other fertility deities. The Israelites frequently fell subject to the temptation of also worshiping Baal, attributing to him the fertility of the land which God had given them. This tragic theology can be seen in the Book of Hosea, especially in chapter 2.

Elijah was a prophet of God. He was not widely accepted. He lived at a time when Ahab and Jezebel were leading the people in the worship of other gods. The worship of Baal and Asherah was widespread. There were 450 prophets who served in the worship of Baal and 400 in the worship of Asherah. Elijah felt that he alone served God. Ahab and Jezebel were greedy individuals. They sought primarily economic prosperity for themselves. They engaged in license and immoral conduct. They sought no one who would oppose them and prevent them from carrying out the goals which they established. For such rulers, a prophet of God was not the appropriate religious companion. They surrounded themselves with individuals who supported their behavior, encouraged them in their greediness, and did not condemn them for violating the statutes and the ordinances of God.

Elijah challenged the prophets of Baal and Asherah to the contest which occurred on Mount Carmel. In that contest, Elijah was vindicated. He destroyed the power of the prophets of Baal and of Asherah. He destroyed the prophets (1 Kings 18:17-29). He sought to break up the synthesis which had occurred between Ahab and Jezebel as political leaders and the false prophets of Baal and Asherah as religious leaders. The civil religion which was perpetuated by Ahab and Jezebel undercut the faith of the people of Israel. Instead of faith in the Lord and obedience to his statutes guiding the people, the people were led astray. Elijah stood as a model for the prophet of God. No stronger denunciation of civil religion can be found than that of Elijah who denounced false worship and called the people to choose which god they would serve.

JEWISH NATIONALISM AND CIVIL RELIGION

Jewish nationalism was a distortion of faith in God. God covenanted with Abraham for obedience and blessing, and promised to give the land to Abraham. The Jewish people, with the passing of time, came to concentrate more upon God's promise of the land to them than upon his requirement of obedience from them. By the time of Jesus, their nationalism had gone through many stages and had experienced many setbacks, but was still a strong, driving force among the people. I have chosen to illustrate this Jewish nationalism with only two passages. But many more could be found.

One of the most obvious passages dealing with civil religion and nationalism is found in Amos 7. *Amos* was a prophet who lived in Judah and was called by God to go to the Northern Kingdom of Israel and prophesy. He prophesied during the eighth century BC, about forty years before the fall of the Northern Kingdom. He and Hosea give us vivid descriptions of the condition of the Northern Kingdom during this period.

Amos delivered a message of judgment to the Northern Kingdom. At a time when feelings of nationalism were rampant, Amos pronounced a word of judgment upon the people for their sins. His message concerned their idolatry, their social oppression of the poor, and their disregard for God's blessings and his statutes. His message was a clear message of doom. God was bringing judgment upon them to punish them for their sins.

Amos delivered this message broadly in the Northern Kingdom. He addressed rulers. He addressed leading citizens. He addressed religious leaders.

Amos even had the audacity to deliver his message of judgment at Bethel. Bethel was the sanctuary where the king and other important persons went to worship. It was well attended by religious persons who served the king and cared for his interests. One such religious leader was Amaziah, the priest of Bethel. Amaziah said to Amos, "O seer, go, flee away to the land of Judah, and eat bread there, and prophesy there; but never again prophesy at Bethel, for it is the king's sanctuary, and it is a temple of the kingdom" (Amos 7:12-13, RSV). Amaziah made clear to Amos that the sanctuary at Bethel was the sanctuary of the king, not the temple of God. The ultimate authority at Bethel was the king, not God. Amaziah perhaps thought that in serving the king he was serving God. But Amaziah neglected to follow the lesson of King David, who responded in repentance to the message of Nathan. In the theocracy which God had established, even the king was to be open to rebuke for his sins. David, when rebuked by Nathan, repented and accepted the judgment which God brought upon him. But this was not to be true at Bethel. At Bethel no voice of dissent was to be heard. No word of criticism of the king's policies would be heard. Only those things which would be pleasing to the king would be heard.

Amaziah had a vested interest in preventing words of criticism.

As priest at the king's sanctuary, he lived a life of prestige, honor, and luxury. He wanted to maintain that position. He stood to lose that position if he incurred the king's disfavor. The way to keep the king's favor was to keep the sanctuary free of criticism of the king.

Jeroboam was king of the Northern Kingdom at a time of prosperity. National sentiments and confidence were high. He wanted to maintain things as they were. The wealthy individuals were prospering. The poor and weak individuals were either silent or unable to create problems for him. Jeroboam lived a life of luxury and satisfaction comparable to that of Pharaoh in the time of Moses. The people of the Northern Kingdom had a religious heritage. One way of maintaining the status quo was to perpetuate religious ritual and religious ceremony which served his political and economic objectives. While some of the people might be concerned if gods other than the Lord were widely worshiped, most of the people would tolerate a form of worship which posed few demands and which offered the appearance of God's blessings for the king's actions. Jeroboam profited greatly from this religion which existed to confer blessings upon the king. Amaziah and the other religious leaders profited greatly from this civil religion, which called upon them to serve as puppets who would pronounce God's blessings upon the king.

Neither the political nor the religious life of the people of the Northern Kingdom served those purposes which God sought for the people. Within a matter of forty years, God would bring judgment upon this distorted form of the theocracy which supposedly existed to serve both God and the nation. The nationalism seen in the Northern Kingdom at the time of Amos was a perversion of the covenant faith. It exalted the nation to the place reserved for the Lord. National goals and the aspirations of the leading citizens were given primary importance. Other concerns were secondary. Concerns for abiding by the moral and social commands given by God were minimal. The conduct to be found in the Northern Kingdom was shocking, but it was blasphemous when it occurred in a nation supposedly acknowledging God as king and with the blessings of the religious leaders. This nationalism was both a perversion of the covenant faith and an intermingling of elitist politics and self-serving religion.

One of the passages with the strongest nationalistic overtones is Psalm 137. This psalm from the Babylonian captivity reflects the deep-seated belief that the covenant faith could not be practiced apart from Jerusalem and the land surrounding it. The psalm reflects the setting of the sixth century BC and the Babylonian Captivity. The people of Judah had been carried into captivity by the Babylonians and were in a land which was foreign to them. They had been humiliated by the destruction of the Temple, the city walls, their dwellings, and the devastation of their land. This conflicted with everything which they believed about God's protection of them and their land.

At this stage in the history of the people of Israel, nationalistic feelings had become so strong that they could not conceive of God's fulfilling his covenant promises without their presence in the land. They completely neglected God's required obedience of Abraham and all successive generations. As a result of this warped theology, they were unable to explain the captivity and their presence in Babylon.

The question of the psalmist is a haunting question: "How shall we sing the Lord's song in a foreign land?" (Ps. 137:4, RSV). The psalmist continues the lament by describing how dear Jerusalem is and his inability to think of worshiping God in Babylon. This form of nationalism identifies faith in God with a particular place. This nationalism does not understand that God's purposes are bigger than Jerusalem. The longing for a land in which to live is both a natural human instinct and an understandable part of the Abrahamic covenant. But God's covenant with

Abraham was bigger than the land of Palestine. It was bigger than Jerusalem. It will always be bigger than any particular place. When one nation or one city or one geographical region becomes so identified with God that God cannot be worshiped elsewhere, nationalism has replaced covenant faith. Nationalism has become the faith of the people.

Nationalism was not restricted to the Old Testament. It is found throughout the Gospels. Jesus, in his frequent encounters with the Jewish religious leaders, resisted the types of false nationalism being espoused by those leaders. I believe that one reason he was rejected by the Jewish people was because he did not accept the type of nationalism that they expressed. As the crucifixion neared, Pilate offered the people their choice of whom he would release to them. Jesus was one alternative: Jesus, the Prince of peace, the one who had resisted efforts to make him king. The other was Barabbas. Barabbas was probably a Zealot. Luke recognizes him as an insurrectionist (Luke 23:18-19). The religious leaders stirred up the people to request Barabbas. They preferred the release of an insurrectionist, with nationalistic tendencies, to a man of peace who placed faith in God and obedience to God above nationalistic aspirations.

JEWISH HEDONISM AND CIVIL RELIGION

This brief treatment of civil religion in the Bible can be concluded by describing the way in which the religion of the people supported the hedonism so prevalent in government and society. A brief treatment will suffice to illustrate this point.

Again, Amos serves as a worthy example. He describes the way in which justice has been distorted by the elders and the rulers who should preserve justice. The systems of justice are weighted to the benefit of the wealthy and the affluent. They trample upon the poor. They live lives of luxury. They do so at the expense of those whom they rob and cheat (Amos 5:10-11). They do so at the very time that they are being outwardly religious by going to sanctuaries such as Bethel and Gilgal. They engage in a form of worship which allows them to continue their evil ways without rebuking them and challenging them to repentance.

The time of the prophet Amos was a time of extreme affluence. The society of the Northern Kingdom was divided into two groups: the affluent and the poor. The affluent maintained their positions by oppressing the poor, by distorting justice, and by depriving the poor of protection and assistance called for by God's laws. The affluent and the religious and political leaders maintained their positions amidst an outward show of religious devotion. But for these people, the most important thing in life was wealth and luxury. Wealth and luxury had become their god. The God of the covenant who demanded justice and righteousness was of secondary importance to the stone houses, luxurious couches, fine foods, and imported clothes with which they adorned themselves. The government was controlled by the affluent. The religion of the Northern Kingdom encouraged perpetuation of this distorted form of religion and government.

Civil religion almost inevitably winds up supporting the wealthy and the affluent in their position in life. In seeking to maintain the status quo, that which civil religion supports is the leadership and the policies of those who are powerful and who control the economic fortunes of the nation. This civil religion supports neglect of the poor and the needy and offers words of consolation to salve any pangs of conscience which might be felt. How far this is from the prophet Amos, the prophet Micah, the prophet Hosea, and others of God's true spokesmen.

CHARACTERISTICS OF CIVIL RELIGION

After examining illustrations of civil religion in the Bible, I will now identify several characteristics of civil religion. Since the purpose of this book is primarily to examine the teachings of the

Bible, I will not devote as much space to contemporary illustrations. It will be helpful, however, to mention some possible manifestations of civil religion.

Civil religion is a form of idolatry which gives unqualified allegiance to some cause, some ideology, or some political institution instead of to the Lord God. I use the word *idolatry* because any loyalty which gives supreme allegiance to anything other than God is idolatry. Idolatry is far more than the worship of some other supposed supernatural being. Idolatry is living life in a manner that fails to assign God his proper place and giving his place to something else instead. One of the most frequent forms of civil religion is found in countries ruled by authoritarian governments which use religion as a means of securing support and cooperation from the people. Authoritarian governments tolerate no rivalry for the allegiance of their citizens. Religion, political persuasion, and ethnic differences are all subordinated to the greater cause of unifying the citizens by whatever means are necessary to secure cooperation.

But authoritarian governments are not the only illustrations that can be given. Western culture is also beset by the temptation to engage in civil religion. The spirit of nationalism can become a dominating ideal that subordinates religion to the role of supporting a particular culture or a particular political system. This happens frequently in times of war. In World War I, supposedly Christian nations engaged in military battle against each other. Germans, Englishmen, Frenchmen, and Americans all went to battle confident that God was supporting their positions in the war. God is not that diverse in his commitments and his loyalties.

One of the greatest rivalries to Christianity is the materialism which has been growing in our culture for several decades. This manifests itself in hedonism, in extravagant affluence, and in the domination of society and government by economic concerns.

Materialism has had a creeping influence in the churches of America, which have become preoccupied by signs of worldly success. When Christianity is invoked to support a particular system of government or a particular system of economics, civil religion is being practiced. God is active in all nations and works in all economic systems.

Civil religion represses and ignores the prophetic role of Christianity to pronounce God's word of judgment upon sin. Where the prophetic tradition of judgment and criticism is lacking, authentic Christianity is missing. In the Old Testament, God raised up the prophets to be his voices in opposing the sins of the rulers, the leading citizens, and the entire nation. The prophets directed the vast majority of their denouncements against those in power who misused their power. In the New Testament, Jesus identified with the prophetic tradition. John the Baptist was an example. No power was great enough to escape the voice of judgment, whether from Paul or John or the other writers. Any position which seeks to mute the voice of criticism, rooted in clear biblical values, opposes authentic Christianity.

In the United States politicians recognize the power and the influence of the churches. Political campaigners constantly seek ways of influencing the different religious communities to gain their support. Christians who are involved in society will naturally be involved in the political process, in party politics, and in evaluating those who seek support. Support can never be given in such a manner that the possibility of speaking a prophetic word is forfeited. In those times when churches have been most powerful and successful in their alliances with governments, the prophetic ideal has been most weakened and ignored.

A tendency is very apparent in the United States. Clergy and involved Christians who give their support to political leaders usually become their defenders. The Christian can never give total support to any political leader. Christians are as a general rule to obey the state. But at times the higher loyalty due to God requires disagreement with political rulers.

The prophetic role can be forfeited quietly and gradually. It can be lost through pride resulting from a visit to the White House or a meeting with an important government official. The prophetic role can be forfeited by smugness from frequent calls seeking assistance. Being praised by leaders of state for being a "key man in the church" may be the first step in becoming a servant of the politicians. There are many Amaziahs who have lived since the time of Amos.

Civil religion seeks to manipulate religion for the purposes of the state. A danger of a close relationship between religion and the state is for the state to manipulate the religious institutions for political reasons. This is another way in which the prophetic role of Christians can be compromised.

Historically, since the time of Constantine, the church in most places has been united to the state. At times the church has dominated. But most of the time the church has been subordinate to the state. This robs the church of its power.

In Europe the pattern of church-state relationship continues as in the time of the founding of the United States. Tax money supports religious causes. Decisions regarding religious matters frequently require government approval. Where government controls religious institutions in that manner, it is easy for the state to manipulate the churches.

Manipulation of churches in the United States is not that easy. Religious liberty and separation of church and state help the churches maintain their independence. While clear delineation of those principles is difficult, we have much greater freedom than do European churches. Independence is necessary for freedom.

A more subtle form of manipulation is practiced on churches in the United States. Prayers at political events often give the form of religion without much substance. Some religious ceremonies are often so nonsectarian that they are inoffensive to almost everyone.

Efforts are frequently made to get Christians and other religious groups to vote in blocks, following the leadership of a few individuals, or deciding on the basis of several key issues. Protestants, Catholics, and Jews are discussed as groups likely to vote in mass for the candidate that ascertains what select sensitive issues sway them. In the minds of some politicians, Christians are merely one more group to be courted. Promises are often made or implied. Christians and other religious groups who lightly accept this type of overture are agreeing to be manipulated in return for some preferential treatment.

Christians are to transform the political order, not to be absorbed by it.

Civil religion becomes resistant to change in politics. Civil religion inevitably becomes a part of the status quo and seeks to maintain it. Those who learn to enjoy power and fraternization with the powerful do not want to lose their privileged status. When times of change are needed, civil religion becomes an obstacle rather than a catalyst.

Things change in politics. Life is dynamic and changing. Political systems must change to meet the needs of changing times. Charles Finney and the abolitionist movement understood that change in the institution of slavery was needed. Many preachers in the South did not see that need and helped reinforce resistance to change on the part of the South.

The God of the Bible is constantly pressing for change. He wanted Abraham to move. He wanted Moses to get involved. He disturbed Elijah's retreat. Jesus was the greatest radical of his day. He ate with sinners, talked with a Samaritan woman, and interacted with Romans. He commended Mary for wanting to be instructed like the men, and urged Martha not to be bound by her traditional role.

Not all things are new. Sometimes things seem to change too quickly. But the Christian is free—free to stay the same and free to change. The Christian finds direction and motivation ultimately in God. Civil religion will rob the Christian of this freedom.

Civil religion neglects the unimportant members of society. Perhaps the greatest harm done by civil religion results from its disregard of the unimportant members of society. In the Old Testament they were widows, orphans, the poor, the weak, and the strangers.

In the United States and the world of today, they remain the same. There are more kinds of orphans—orphans of war, of neglect, and of death. The weak may be the sick, the hungry, or the nonwhite members of society.

Civil religion identifies itself with the powerful, the wealthy, the elite. It wants little to do with those who are unimportant. They are dirty, smelly, and have problems. They are of value at times of voting and taking pictures. Otherwise, things go better if they stay with their "own kind."

The gospel was and is good news to all people: the Pharisee and the publican, the Jew and the Gentile, the rich man and the pauper. Jesus could have lived with the leaders of society. But their rejection of the unimportant individuals was a part of the Jewish rejection of his messianic mission.

No greater test of the Christian influence on society can be found than in that society's treatment of its unimportant. To be Christian means to feed the hungry, to give drink to the thirsty, to give clothes to the naked, and to visit those in prison (Matt. 25:31-46). Any expression of Christianity which does not do this is not following the command of Jesus. Any government which does not do this has not been penetrated by the transforming power of the gospel.

7.
Christian Values and Public Policy

Here I hope to describe how Christians have been involved in some major political issues. Then, I want to make some suggestions for political involvement. I will focus on some of the functions government is to perform which were identified in earlier chapters.

There are many values which Christians should work for in society. I have chosen to focus on peace, justice, and compassion. I think these values are at the heart of the Christian responsibility in society. I think they grow more clearly out of the biblical teachings than other values and therefore require prior consideration.

One thing to remember is what the Bible teaches. It teaches us basic values which are to be followed. It does not give us specific strategies on how to implement these values in government. These, Christians must devise in each generation.

PEACE

One of the functions of government which was identified in the treatment of the Old Testament is the defense of the nation from its enemies and the establishment of peace. The kings of Israel were judged in part by their success or failure in defending the nation from its enemies. In the New Testament, Paul enjoyed the peace achieved by Rome's political domination. One of the most basic responsibilities of any government is the defense of its citizens.

One of the most difficult problems confronted by Christians over the centuries is the problem of war.[1] It is such a recurring problem that reflection upon it is usually set in the negative terms of conflict, not the mandate for peace. We usually talk about whether or not war is moral. We look at different theories of justifying war. We too often forget that the end to be achieved is peace, not domination or conquest. War can possibly secure the absence of violent conflict. Whether or not it achieves peace is another matter.

Jesus is the Prince of Peace. He chose not to use physical force to save his own life. He taught about peace among men. He taught that his disciples were to follow the way of peace.

The early church was pacifist. Space does not allow an examination of how the position of the church was changed. The changing fortunes of the church in Roman political life had much to do with the change in attitude toward Christian involvement in the military.

Pacifism has remained one of the attitudes toward war in the Christian tradition, but it is not the main one. Pacifism is opposed to war under all circumstances. It has been championed by many groups. Currently the Quaker and Mennonite traditions are primary advocates of the pacifist position. This belief has often been expressed in the form of conscientious objection to involvement in war. The United States government has recognized the moral legitimacy of a sincere claim to be a conscientious objector for individuals opposed to war for serious religious or moral reasons.

One of the defenses of war which has frequently been made is referred to as the *holy war* theory. This viewpoint is the oldest justification of war. Those who have held this view have asserted that a particular war is being fought to achieve the purposes of a particular deity. Usually those who advocate the theory of a holy war identify the will of God with the national will of the people. The Crusades tended to be holy wars, with both Christians and Moslems believing they were fighting for the glory of their respective deities. In modern life, the theory of holy war is most clearly demonstrated by the perspective associated with the Moslem resurgence in Iran.

The third major position on war is the *just war* theory. This is the theory usually associated with a Christian defense of military involvement. The theory was developed in the fourth and fifth centuries. A war was considered just if it met several qualifications. It must be a war between legitimate rulers and countries, not a revolution. The war must be fought for some just reason, some moral cause. The means by which the war was fought had to be just or legitimate. Excessive force could not be morally justified. A reasonable possibility of accomplishing the just cause must exist.

Christians have been involved in many wars. Many Christians supported the Revolution for independence from England. The Civil War was marked by religious support on both sides. A mood of isolationism and slight pacifism marked the pre-World War II era. But Christians in the United States gave strong support to the battle for freedom.

The Vietnam War was probably the most controversial in our nation's history. There were more voices of protest against this undeclared war than any war the United States has fought. There were a number of reasons for this. Serious question was raised about the objectives for which the war was being fought. Doubts were also raised about the legitimacy of the weapons with which the war was fought. The citizens of the United States were sensitized to the terrible power of weapons with the use of the atomic bomb in World War II. Television cameras and photographers for newspapers and magazines captured the horror of death of both Americans and Vietnamese. The pathos of war provoked both religious and nonreligious individuals and groups to protest the war.

Most Christians who regard a particular war as moral have usually done so from the perspective of a just war theory. Most who do so regard war as being an occasional tragic possibility of human sinfulness. Most who accept the just war theory regard a pacifist position as too idealistic.

The 1980s are a time for continued debate about war and peace. The Falkland Islands War and the Israeli invasion of Lebanon demonstrate how delicate the international balance is. The United States and Russia are involved in massive expenditures for weapons which can literally destroy mankind. Beginning in late 1981, a wave of protest swept Europe and grew in the United States. Political opportunists and propagandizers of many persuasions were involved and used the protest movement. But hundreds of thousands of concerned citizens, many of them Christians, began to express major concerns about the fate of mankind.

Christians certainly would be among the last people to want to be conquered by an authoritarian regime. But, hopefully, Christians will be asking important questions in the days ahead.

The major question is how peace can be achieved. Without being naive and idealistic in the extreme, Christians will ask questions about securing peace, not winning wars. Defense and military preparedness are necessary steps for a bigger concern: peace among men.

How many weapons are needed? This question will continue to haunt those engaged not only in the military but also in deciding how our government spends its money. Will more weapons increase our safety? Are the weapons we have the right kinds of weapons? Great Britain had nuclear capabilities. But it took weeks for Great Britain to secure a military resolution to the Falkland Islands crisis with conventional weapons. If we are genuinely interested in defense, do we need as many nuclear weapons as we have? These questions are complicated military questions, but they are also political questions. For the military policy of our government should reflect some sense of public opinion about the arms race, sale of weapons to other nations, and the threat of nuclear war.

A closely related issue is the issue of military spending. Our government is embarked on a program of military buildup. The cost will be enormous. Imagine a nation spending one million dollars per day, beginning with the birth of Jesus and continuing until today. That nation would have spent less than one half the money that the United States is scheduled to spend on defense in the next five years! Surely there is another way. The costs to our "enemies" are just as great.

Can we continue to talk about war being "just" in a nuclear age? One of the qualifications for the just war theory has been the requirement that the means of fighting the war be just. How are nuclear weapons "just"? The destruction which they produce is enormous. Some scientists say that a large nuclear bomb will produce temperatures ranging as high as thirty million degrees Fahrenheit. The resulting damage would be enormous. Medical facilities and medication would be destroyed. The "survivors" could look forward to a life of pain, physical degeneration, and genetic mutation. We cannot begin to understand how horrible this is.

These are not answers. They are questions the Christian must answer in taking seriously the Bible's claim that peace is the goal for society.

JUSTICE

Another function of government which is germane for our consideration is the promotion of justice and fairness. This concern, identified in the Old Testament, was carried over in the

New Testament in Paul's treatment of government in Romans 13. Rulers are not a terror to good works but to bad. Those who do good are to be encouraged by government.

The United States government has justice as a central concern for its structure and its action. The United States Constitution and its Bill of Rights sought to establish a form of government which would be just in its treatment of its citizens and treat them fairly. In the guarantee of the rights of life, liberty, and the pursuit of happiness, this government sought to establish protection from arbitrary restrictions and unwarranted limitations upon human freedom.

The structure of our government reflects a concern for justice and fairness. The different branches of our government distribute the power of government among three different branches. Total power is not vested in any one branch of government or any one individual, because of our realization that any person, any institution, is capable of failure. Moods change dramatically in our nation. Public opinion can change quickly. The possibility always exists that the rights of individuals and groups can be trampled upon in the heat of emotion. The series of checks and balances built into our government sought to make changes in basic rights slowly and with careful consideration. Such deliberation prevents sudden changes in public opinion from becoming oppressive of minority groups and unpopular individuals.

Concepts such as justice and equality have changed as our nation has matured. When this nation was founded, the only voting citizens were free, white males. Gradually our nation has changed. Equality before the law means equality of participation for former slaves, nonwhites, and women—without regard to property ownership. No nation has afforded a higher degree of participation to its citizens. The process has been long and is not yet completed. But the concern for justice and fairness has caused monumental change in American politics.

Justice is a concept which is difficult to define adequately. Therefore, it means different things to different individuals. Freedom is not absolute. The rights of free speech, free press, free association, and freedom of religion are not to be denied, but they may be regulated for the benefit of the entire society. An individual cannot drive through residential streets late at night, broadcasting religious beliefs over a loudspeaker in such a manner that the peace of the neighborhood is disturbed. The rights of the residents are as valid as the right to freedom of religion. The right is secure even though the manner of exercising it may be limited.

One area in the struggle for justice in which Christians have played a leading role is the area of civil rights. This is not surprising when the abolitionist movement of the nineteenth century is remembered. Although many Southern preachers were actively defending the institution of slavery, the abolitionist movement was fueled by preachers such as Charles Finney. The concern for equality and freedom expressed there surfaced again strongly in the 1950s and 1960s with the realization that the goals of freedom and equality had not yet been achieved.

The thrust of the civil rights movement was the liberation of blacks from cultural and political situations of inequality. Black churchmen such as Martin Luther King, Jr., sought liberation from economic impoverishment and political alienation. The economic and political sectors of life in the United States were clearly restrictive and limited in their openness to blacks. Educational institutions had continued to be segregated for almost a century after the abolition of slavery. The resulting inequality of education served to perpetuate the class structure of racial separation.

Many white churchmen participated in the struggle. Christians from many denominations joined in the struggle. Many of the agencies discussed in the chapter on religious organizations and public policy worked extensively for expansion of civil rights for blacks.

The struggle for justice and equal opportunity for individuals of all races continues. The United States is increasingly a multiethnic nation. The fastest growing ethnic group in the United States is the Hispanic population. Political oppression in Asia and Latin America have caused literally millions of individuals to seek refuge in this nation. The enormous responsibility of remaining the melting pot, the land of the free, is one of the greatest challenges of our nation's future.

The gospel requires that Christians take this challenge seriously. In Christ there is neither Jew nor Gentile. We are all equal in God's eyes. This does not mean exactness of identity, but equality of opportunity and participation. This equality is a goal for Christians and any others in our society with whom Christians can work.

Another illustration of the challenge of securing justice can be seen in the field of criminal justice. The need for society to protect its citizens from criminals is apparent. Paul, in Romans 13, said that only evildoers had cause to fear good government. A goal of social organization is the elimination of force being used widely to settle disputes. Our system was established so that disputes would be settled by the courts.

According to the Department of Justice, at the end of 1981 about one out of every eighty-three adults in the United States was either in prison or on some form of release program.

The problem of justice in our criminal system is a staggering one. Society must be protected. The persons against whom crime is perpetrated need various forms of protection. The rights of the accused must not be ignored because of the emotions of the moment or some supposed expediency.

Perhaps the area of criminal justice is the one in which the rights of the individual and the rights of society have proved the most difficult to balance. The courts have seldom evoked more ire than when they have protected the right to a fair trial of individuals accused of unpopular crimes.

A pattern still exists in our society. Those who are affluent and can afford to hire teams of skilled attorneys and to continue procedural appeals seldom serve major prison sentences. Most of the inhabitants of prisons continue to be poor and of ethnic minority heritage.

Reform of the criminal justice system is a very complicated problem. Christians have begun to take seriously the necessity of establishing prison ministries to speak to the spiritual needs of the inmates. But justice continues to be a haunting goal. Our society is capable of reacting strongly to crises such as rising crime rates. Christians should be active in the process of reform to prevent the field of criminal justice from losing redemptive purposes for the individual. When punishment is called for, it should not be excessive and vengeful. Prisoners should not be treated like animals. The image of prisoners enjoying a good life of luxury is simply without foundation in fact. A visit to a jail or a prison will dispel that myth.

The demands of justice are monumental. They are impossible to adequately define. For the Christian, a first step is to follow the Golden Rule given by Jesus. We are to treat others, to establish our society, as we would be treated, and have our society treat us.

Another challenge to our entire society is the restraint of those who are powerful. The Christian should never forget the story of David and Nathan. David was one of the mightiest rulers of his time. Yet he sinned by committing adultery and arranging for the killing of Bathsheba's husband. In the Old Testament, the king was a ruler who was to be subject to the same moral and civil laws as others. Nathan, a prophet of God, declared to David God's judgment that not even a mighty king can act without restraint.

Even in the Old Testament, with the king supposedly ruling as God's representative, God found it necessary to use prophets to declare to the kings that they were not free to act without restraint. The weak and the poor are not to be at the whim of the powerful.

Jesus followed the model of the Old Testament prophets. He confronted evil at every hand. He spoke out strongly against the leading citizens of Judaism—the Sadducees and the Pharisees—time after time. He regarded them as part of an oppressive system which conferred upon them economic favors and prestige, at the expense of the commoners.

Our age is one which is becoming increasingly materialistic. Economic concerns and values are having an enormous effect upon the values being pursued in the political arena. Party affiliation, causes for which concern is being expressed, and goals to be achieved through government action are greatly affected by economic concerns. I firmly believe that one of the greatest dangers confronting our society is the danger of becoming a society of economic classes. Perhaps we already are that kind of society. But the degree to which it may be happening is frightening. Many of the revolutions in history which have occurred have been revolutions against an alliance of religious institutions and the affluent members and groups of society.

Materialism is not simply an external enemy of the church. Churches and Christians are being influenced by materialistic tendencies whenever worldly standards of success become more important than God's priorities. And in God's eyes, wealth can become so important to a person that it becomes a god. The encounter Jesus had with the rich young ruler is a very contemporary story.

Responsible stewardship of God's gifts is the subject for another study. But it certainly means that we will not consent to a system of government in which those who are wealthy are able to accomplish their goals without regard for the rest of society.

COMPASSION

Both the Old Testament and the New Testament are very specific about the need for compassion in dealing with those who are not strong. The civil laws which God established to guide the nation of Israel provided very specific protection for them. God promised that he would reward faithfulness and punish disobedience. Leviticus 25 and 26 spell out vividly the judgment which God would visit upon the nation if these civil laws were ignored. It is ironic that some who would seek to imitate the theocratic model of government ignore this emphasis in the Bible.

The ministry of Jesus abounds with illustrations of his concern for the weak and the poor. He regarded this concern as a model to be followed by all who were his disciples. He also cautioned soldiers on how they were to perform their duty. Zacchaeus was a tax collector who was given very specific advice on how he was to handle his responsibility. The ultimate challenge of meeting the needs of the poor was given to the rich young ruler. These passages, so familiar to us, abound with political meaning. Those who govern are to do so compassionately.

The government of the United States was established, among other things, to guarantee "life, liberty, and the pursuit of happiness." This phrase is a modification of a phrase from John Locke, the English philosopher who profoundly affected the founding fathers. He spoke of life, liberty, and property. Although the phrase was changed, property is included in this "pursuit of happiness."

Locke lived in pre-industrial England in the seventeenth century. The founding fathers of the eighteenth century were quite familiar with him. Locke was widely quoted for his political philosophy, inasmuch as his concept of limited government and government through social contract shaped the United States Constitution.

I want to emphasize an economic aspect of his thought which I think is helpful for our consideration of compassion for the poor. One passage from Locke seems to me especially important:

> The Labour of his Body, and the Work of his Hands, we may say, are properly his. Whatsoever then he removes out of the State that Nature hath provided, and left it in, of that mixed his Labour with, and joyned to it something that is his own, and thereby makes it his Property. It being by him removed from the common state Nature placed it in, hath by this labour something annexed to it, that excludes the common right of other Men. For this Labour being the unquestionable Property of the Labourer, no Man but he can have a right to what that is once joyned to, at least where there is enough, and as good left in common for others.[2]

In this quote, Locke emphasizes two things that I think are particularly important. First, a person acquired property in that agricultural setting through subduing it or acquiring it through his labor. This point still is accepted in our system although the manner in which work appropriates it is different for many people. We now have a monetary system, based largely upon industry, through which we think of property differently.

The second emphasis in the quote is the right to an amount of property and the expectation that it will be sufficient in quantity and quality. This language expresses the belief that there is an inherent right to property possessed by everyone. Like all rights, there are qualifications on the extent to which that right is exercised.

Government has the responsibility of protecting property rights. Few points of our nation's history are clearer. This usually has taken the form of legislation to encourage and develop business. Frequently tariffs have been used to provide some form of protection for American businesses. Recently legislation has attempted to provide necessary regulation to protect the rights of businesses and individuals and to ensure that the needs of the general population are cared for.

A more recent debate has been the role of government in assuring the property needs of individuals. Here I mean property needs in very broad terms. Food, shelter, and clothing are items of personal property needed for a minimum standard of living. Until the Depression of the 1930s, most individual property needs were cared for adequately by work and charitable institutions. The unemployment and economic collapse of the Depression presented such enormous problems that the basic human property needs of masses of people could not be cared for without government action.

Growth has occurred in the many ways in which our government has attempted in recent decades to care for the personal needs of disadvantaged citizens. The present economic crisis has been the occasion for rethinking the role of government in the whole area of social services. Few social problems are more complex and have aroused more emotion. I do not offer a simple solution to such a complex problem.

Several suggestions can be offered for the Christian who wants to work to make our government compassionate in caring for its citizens. The first suggestion is that government which seeks to perform a valid function *must* take seriously this responsibility. The Christian understands the heritage of the Old Testament and its demand for compassion for the weak and the poor. In the New Testament, Jesus identified with the poor and the outcast in their needs and spoke of the way in which our treatment of them reflects our commitment to God and constitutes the criterion by which we will be judged (Matt. 25).

Second, we cannot separate our private actions from our public actions. We are as responsible for actions in the political realm as we are in the private regions of our life. It is a moral imperative to care for the needy in our personal action. It is equally imperative that in our involvement in politics we seek to achieve the same liberation from want and deprivation. In a political society, the actions of government are to be oriented toward such humanitarian causes as feeding the hungry, caring for women and children in need, and helping the sick and elderly. Christians cannot be blameless if our government becomes insensitive to such needs.

Third, we cannot solve the problem by definition. We often become too concerned about defining who is truly needy and worthy. This can become the same type of avoidance being practiced by the lawyer who asked Jesus, "And who is my neighbor?" (Luke 10:29, RSV). The lawyer sought to avoid the obvious responsibility of caring for the needy by defining who is worthy to receive our help. We can be overcome by the complexity of the problem and seek to avoid it by defining who is worthy and sufficiently needy.

Fourth, we need to work for policies which will enhance the feelings of worth and responsibility in our citizens. One criticism of some recent social service programs is that they tend to encourage continued dependence on others. If that is true, the policies need to be changed. Our society needs to provide sufficient opportunities for individuals so that they will have both the incentive and opportunity to be independent. Christian stewardship requires that we avoid wasting resources. In a world of finite resources, we must learn to make our resources serve as many needs as possible.

Fifth, we must be careful that criticisms of social service programs are not a form of materialism and greed. There are those who criticize government aid to the needy and poor because they have no desire to help others. Some of them are motivated by materialistic desires that simply want to avoid any expense that can be avoided. A good test is to see whether the individual opposing the programs offers an alternative on how the problem can be solved and plans realistically for the financial resources to accomplish the alleviation of human need.

Epilogue

Anticipating how Christians in America will express their faith in political involvement is most difficult. I want to identify some key issues and questions which are extremely important for the coming decade in the area of Christian citizenship.

Perhaps the most important issue is the manner in which Christians deal with the diversity of conclusions which are drawn from the Bible and history about which values are to be stressed and what strategies are to be pursued. While Christian concerns about political issues are quite high at this time, there is a keen awareness of wide diversity of opinions and conclusions. This is demonstrated by the significant differences existing on such matters as school prayer, tuition tax credits, abortion, and the economic role of government. Proponents of both sides of these issues can be found who champion their positions because of strongly held Christian beliefs.

There is a high level of awareness of these differences within the religious community. There are two possible consequences which I fear. One consequence is the possibility of the Christian voice being lost in public circles because of the inability to agree. Media consciousness of the religious communities in the United States is quite high at the present time. Every area of major disagreement will be magnified. This inability to fashion areas of consensus may lead to the image of political involvement by Christians being purely sectarian and a reflection of denominational and theological biases rather than manifestations of commitment to biblical principles. A second consequence is the loss of interest on the part of the average Christian. It is possible that many of those Christians who are now seeking to be involved in politics will cease trying to do so. It is not unusual for groups of individuals to curtail or stop efforts when they reflect an air of controversy and uncertainty. The result would be a "dropping out" of political involvement by Christians.

I would hope that the decade ahead is one which will be marked by an intensive effort on the part of the Christian community in building a consensus, on finding those issues which seem to be most clearly rooted in the teachings of the Bible. Modesty and humility may require that Christians seek to speak on fewer issues and to do so with more clarity.

A second major issue which grows out of the first is the necessity to be more specific about what values are to be applied to society. This is a pluralist society. Many of the individuals of our nation do not choose to use their religious freedom to worship the Lord God. Without diminishing efforts at evangelism within this context, Christians must be aware of the political rights of others. The effort to shape society in a way that reflects Christian values must recognize certain limits. This will require careful thinking about the relationship between Christian values and those held by individuals of other religious traditions or individuals without religious identification.

A third major issue is the question of strategy. How will Christians work for political objectives considered vital to and consistent with the Christian faith? Some signs exist that a realignment may be about to occur in the American political parties. The most likely realignment will be in the conservative political camp. A constant temptation is the formation of a "Christian" political party. I expect that efforts will be made in the decade ahead either to form such a party or to claim that identification for a new political party. Such an issue must be informed by the lessons of history.

The decade ahead promises to be one of the most exciting and challenging in human history. The complexities facing our nation and the world are enormous. The perils facing mankind are monumental. The needs and the crises demand our maximum efforts at making the decades ahead the best possible for future generations. The political arena will continue to be an important area in which major decisions will be made, policies shaped, and future directions charted. May God grant us the courage and perseverance to make the Christian voice heard and the compassion of the gospel embodied in policies and actions, thus making this a better world in which to live.

Notes

Chapter 1.

1. See, e.g., Foy Valentine, *Citizenship for Christians* (Nashville: Broadman Press, 1968), pp. 25-27.

2. Reinhold Niebuhr, *The Children of Light and the Children of Darkness* (New York: Charles Scribner's Sons, 1944), p. xiii.

3. Two helpful articles are: I. Rabinowitz, "Government," and J. W. Wevers, "Theocracy," in *The Interpreter's Dictionary of the Bible,* 1962 ed.

Chapter 3.

1. The manner in which I have organized these categories has been influenced by H. Richard Niebuhr, *Christ and Culture* (New York: Harper & Row, Publishers, 1951).

2. I had written this section before reading Francis A. Schaeffer, *A Christian Manifesto* (Westchester, IL: Crossway Books, 1981), but I am pleased he shares this conclusion on pages 120-121 of his book.

Chapter 4.

1. Albert J. Menendez, "Religious Lobbies," *Liberty* (March/April 1982), pp. 2-5, 20-21.

2. Paul J. Weber, "Examining the Religious Lobbies," *This World* (Winter/Spring 1982), pp. 97-106.

3. Eugene Ebersole, *Church Lobbying in the Nation's Capital* (New York: The Macmillan Company, 1951).

Chapter 5.

1. James E. Wood, Jr., E. Bruce Thompson, and Robert T. Miller, *Church and State* (Waco, TX.: Baylor University Press, 1958), pp. 92-95.

2. P. L. Ford (ed.), *The Writings of Thomas Jefferson* (New York: G. P. Putnam's Sons, 1892), I, 62, quoted in Wood, Thompson, Miller, p. 94.

Suggested Readings in This Area: *Church and State,* published by Americans United for the Separation of Church and State, 8120 Fenton St., Silver Spring, Maryland 20910 (each month except August); *Report from the Capital,* published ten times per year by the Baptist Joint Committee on Public Affairs, 200 Maryland Avenue, N.E., Washington, D.C. 20002.

Chapter 7.

1. The classic historical treatment on the subject is Roland H. Bainton, *Christian Attitudes Toward War and Peace* (New York, Nashville: Abingdon Press, 1960).

2. John Locke, *Two Treatises on Government* (New York: New American Library, 1968, p. 329).